Contents

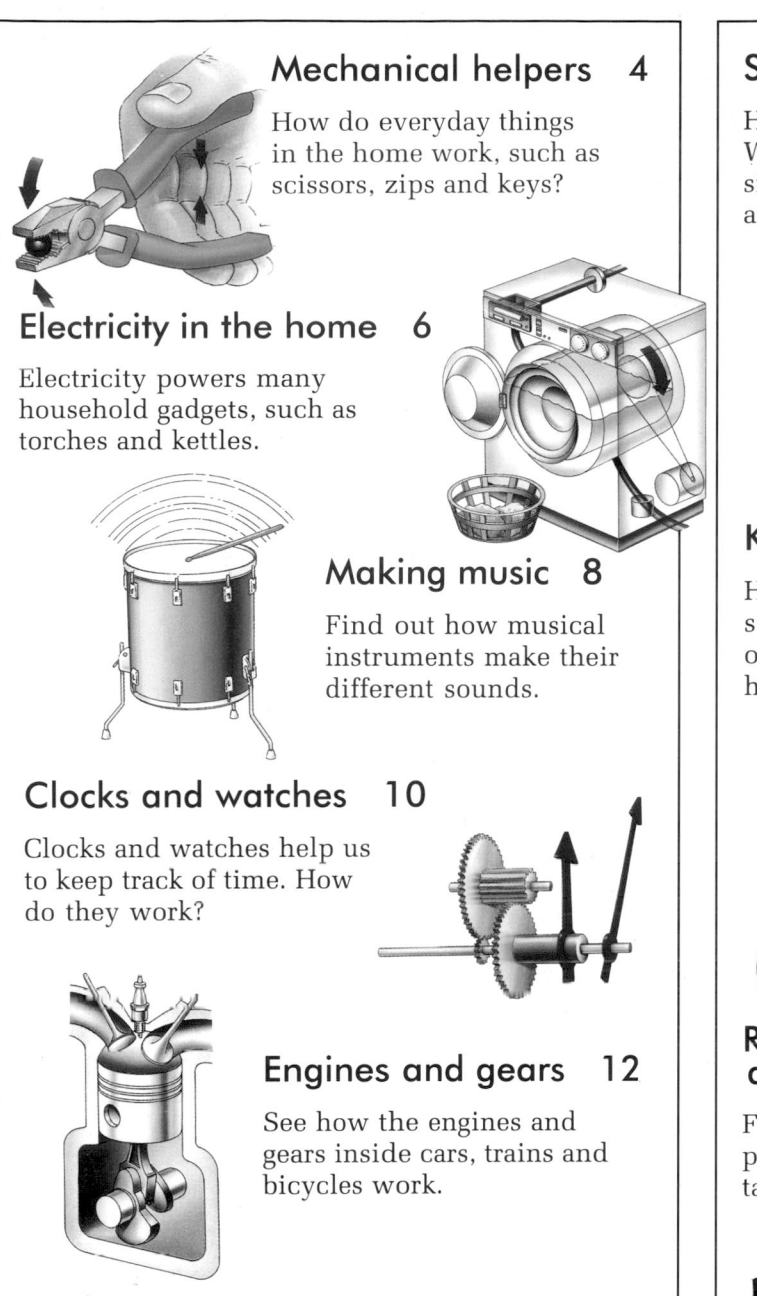

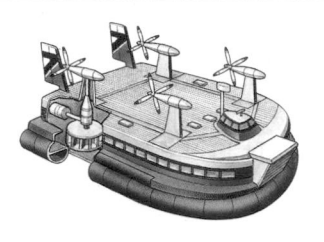

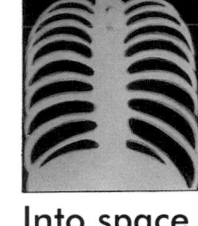
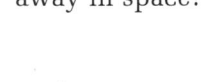

Mechanical helpers

The lever

Many simple tools work using the principle of the lever. A lever is a simple machine which normally makes a force (a push or a pull) larger. The simplest type of lever is a bar which pivots (turns) at a fixed point (called the fulcrum), such as a plank on a log.

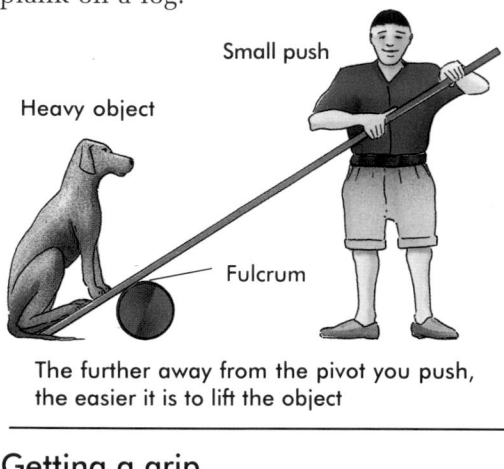

Small push

Heavy object

Fulcrum

The further away from the pivot you push, the easier it is to lift the object

Getting a grip

A pair of pliers is made up of two levers. The two parts are held together by a rotating joint. A small push on the handles forces the grips together with a much larger push.

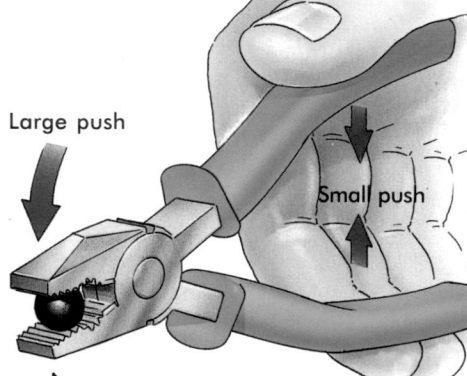

Large push

Small push

Fulcrum

In your everyday life you use many tools and household appliances. Some are very simple and straight forward. Others are much more complex.

A cutting edge

Scissors and other cutting tools, such as garden shears, have two sharp blades. The edges of the blades are pushed across each other by closing the handles together. The nearer to the fulcrum the object is, the easier it is to cut through it. This is because of the lever principle.

Fulcrum

Cutting edge

Gently does it

Instead of letting you grip things tightly, a pair of tweezers lets you grip delicate things gently. This is done by using a special sort of lever that makes a force smaller.

Fulcrum

Push

Smaller push here

3 million BC

Prehistoric people begin to make simple rock hand tools.

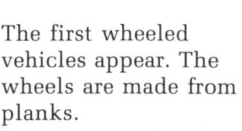

c3500 BC

The first wheeled vehicles appear. The wheels are made from planks.

c3300 BC

Sailing ships with simple square sails are used on the River Nile in Egypt.

Knowledge MASTERS *plus*

HOW THINGS WORK

Written by
Chris Oxlade

Consultants
Dr John Becklake and Sue Becklake

Illustrated by
Mainline Design, Kuo Kang Chen
and John Fox

About this book

Consultants:
Dr John Becklake and
Sue Becklake have
worked for many
years at the Science
Museum in London.
Both have consulted
on a large number of
books for children.

Published in 2002 by
Zigzag, an imprint of
Chysalis Children's
Books,
64 Brewery Road,
London N7 9NT

© 2002 Zigzag
Children's Books

Cover illustrators:
Mainline Design,
Kuo Kang Chen
and John Fox

Concept: Tony Potter
Editors: Kay
Barnham
and Hazel Songhurst

Printed and bound in
China.

ISBN 1-903954-398 (HB)
ISBN 1-903954-436 (PB)

INTERNET LINKS
Every effort has been
made to ensure none
of the recommended
websites in this book is
linked to inappropriate
material. However, due
to the ever-changing
nature of the Internet,
the publishers regret
they cannot take
responsibility for
future content of
these websites.

This book explains how many of the things around us work. Discover what makes clocks tick, light bulbs light up and pictures appear on the television. These and other fascinating topics are explored in clear text and colourful pictures.

INTERNET SAFETY

Internet Links throughout the book allow you to explore topics further, including history-related activities and games. Be sure to follow these guidelines for a fun and safe journey through cyberspace:

1. Ask your parents for permission before you go online.
2. Spend time with your parents online and show them your favourite sites.
3. Post your family's e-mail address, even if you have your own (only give your personal address to someone you trust).
4. Do not reply to e-mails if you feel they are strange or upsetting.
5. Do not use your real surname while you are online.
6. Never arrange to meet 'cyber friends' in person without your parents' permission.
7. Never give out your password.
8. Never give out your home address or telephone number.
9. Do not send scanned pictures of yourself unless your parents approve.
10. Leave a website straight away if you find something that is offensive or upsetting. Talk to your parents about it.

The illustrated Timeline that runs through the book shows you the progress of technology from earliest times to present day. It lists important inventions, developments and people.

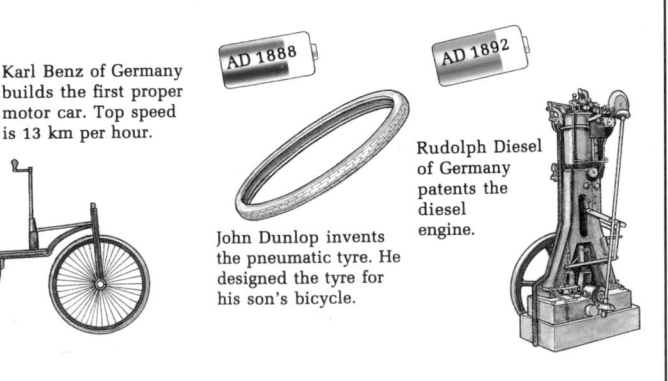

AD 1885 Gottlieb Daimler of Germany tests a petrol engine on a motorcycle.

AD 1885 Karl Benz of Germany builds the first proper motor car. Top speed is 13 km per hour.

AD 1888 John Dunlop invents the pneumatic tyre. He designed the tyre for his son's bicycle.

AD 1892 Rudolph Diesel of Germany patents the diesel engine.

Opening tins

A tin opener is really a combination of two tools. First, there is a scissor-like device which pushes a sharpened steel wheel through the tin's lid. It also grips the tin by its rim. Secondly, turning the handle turns the tin, making the wheel cut around the lid.

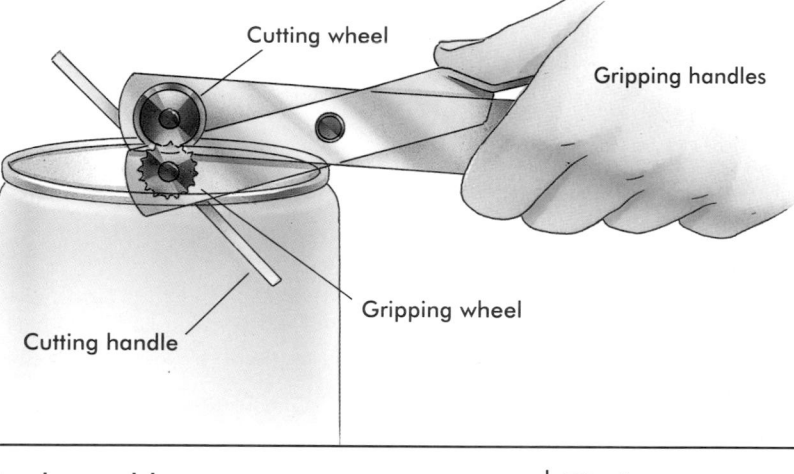

Cutting wheel

Gripping handles

Gripping wheel

Cutting handle

Flushing away

There are two separate parts to a toilet cistern. A floating ball on a lever opens and closes a valve to fill the tank. Pressing the handle forces water from the tank into a pipe which runs down to the toilet bowl. Once the water is flowing it keeps going until the tank is empty. The water flows up the pipe before falling into the toilet bowl. This is called a siphon.

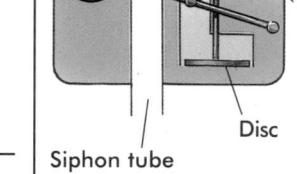

Float   Handle

Valve

Siphon tube   Disc   Toilet flushing

Locks and keys

One of the most common types of lock is called a pin tumbler lock. It is used in doors, padlocks and cars. Inside is a cylinder which is stopped from turning by a row of pins sticking into it. The correct key for the lock lifts the pins so that the cylinder can turn. The turning action pulls back the door bolt, opens the padlock or starts the car.

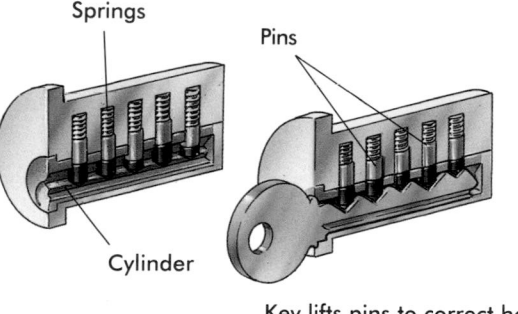

Springs

Pins

Cylinder

Key lifts pins to correct height

Zip fastener

A zip fastener allows two edges to be joined together temporarily. Each edge has a row of teeth which interlock with the teeth on the other edge. The zip-pull guides the teeth together or pulls them apart.

Zip-pull

Wedges guide teeth together

Teeth

Aerosol

Inside an aerosol can are two liquids under pressure — the product (for example, air freshener or hair spray) and the propellant. Pushing the button opens a valve and the pressure pushes the liquids out. The narrow outlet tube makes the liquid break up into a spray. As the liquid is used up, the propellant turns to gas to keep up the pressure.

Outlet tube   Button

Strong can to resist pressure

Spray

Valve

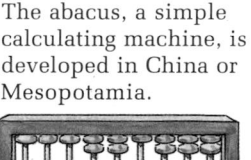
c3000 BC

The abacus, a simple calculating machine, is developed in China or Mesopotamia.

600 BC

The Greeks invent the compound pulley, a machine for lifting heavy weights.

200s BC

Greek mathematician Archimedes invents the Archimedean screw. It lifts water for irrigation.

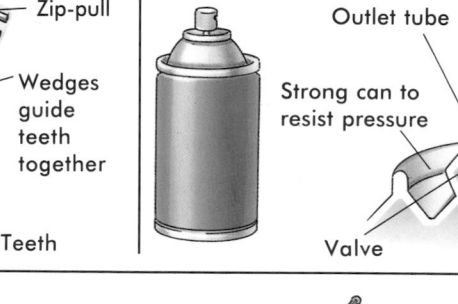

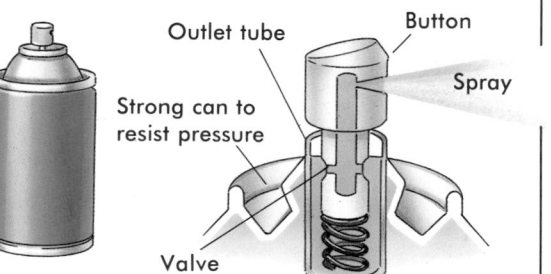

200s BC

Gear wheels are being used in Greece and Egypt.

Electricity in the home

Many of the machines around your home need electricity to make them work. Electricity is used to make lights work, to make motors turn and to heat things up.

Lighting the way

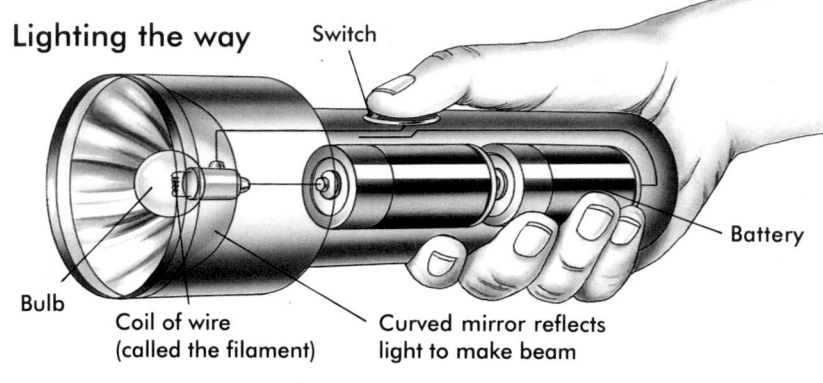

Switch

Battery

Bulb

Coil of wire (called the filament)

Curved mirror reflects light to make beam

One of the simplest electrical devices is the torch. It consists of a battery, a switch and a light bulb. Closing the switch completes the circuit for the electric current to flow from the battery, through the bulb, and back to the battery. Inside the bulb is a coil of very thin wire. When the current flows through this, it makes it very hot — so hot that is glows brightly.

A socket has three wires. Two of them, called live and neutral, are like battery terminals. There is also a safety wire called earth.

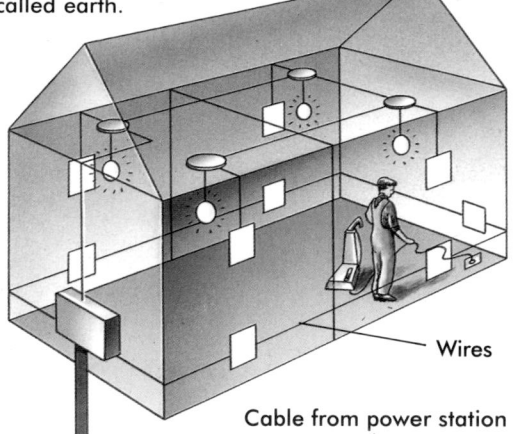

Wires

Cable from power station

Mains electricity

Most electrical things around your home use electricity from the mains. The mains is like a very powerful battery. The electricity is made at a power station and travels to your home along thick cables. Wires carry the electricity around your home to where it's needed.

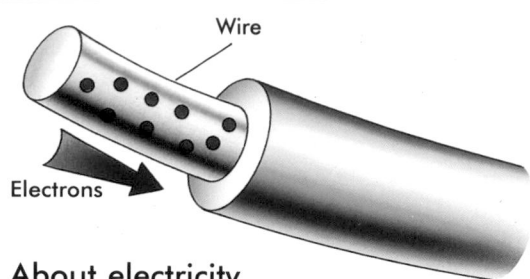

Wire

Electrons

About electricity

Think of an electric current as being like flowing water, and wires like pipes. An electric current flows where there are wires, and it needs something, for example a battery, to push it along the wires. In fact, an electric current is a flow of extremely tiny particles called electrons.

Warming water

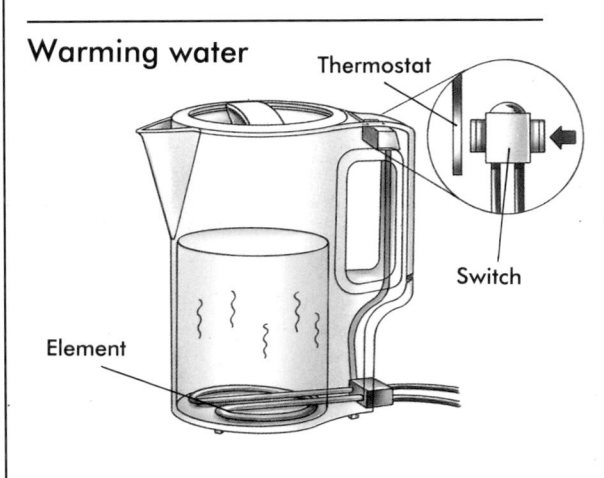

Thermostat

Switch

Element

A kettle uses electricity to heat water. An electric current flows through a special metal strip (called an element) in the bottom of the kettle. A special switch called a thermostat turns the kettle off when the water boils. The steam produced by the boiling water heats the strip, making it bend and turn the switch off.

c200 BC

The Romans invent the hypocaust, a system of under-floor central heating.

AD 60

Hero of Alexandria builds a simple machine that is turned by the power of steam.

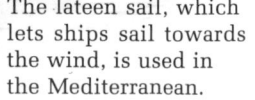

cAD 100s

The lateen sail, which lets ships sail towards the wind, is used in the Mediterranean.

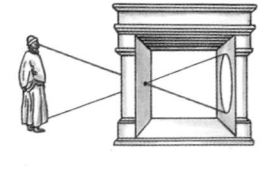

cAD 1000

Arab artists are using a camera obscura — like a huge camera without film.

INTERNET LINK http://www.sciencebob.com
Click on 'Experiments to Choose' and learn how to bend water with static electricity!

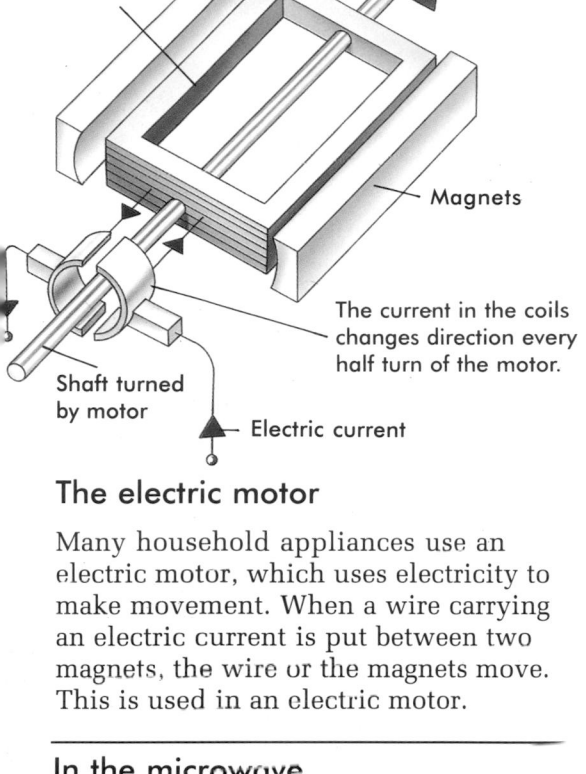

Wire coils

Magnets

The current in the coils changes direction every half turn of the motor.

Shaft turned by motor

Electric current

The electric motor

Many household appliances use an electric motor, which uses electricity to make movement. When a wire carrying an electric current is put between two magnets, the wire or the magnets move. This is used in an electric motor.

In the microwave

Microwaves are similar to the radio waves that your television and radio picks up. When microwaves hit things, they make the tiny particles inside (called molecules) vibrate. This makes the things hot very quickly.

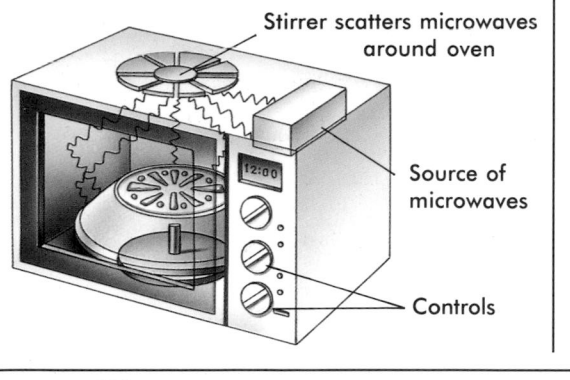

Stirrer scatters microwaves around oven

Source of microwaves

Controls

Washing machine

A washing machine washes, rinses and spins dirty washing. The washing sits in a rotating drum. The drum itself is inside a watertight tank which can be filled with water and pumped dry. The drum is turned slowly during washing and very quickly for drying. The motor, pumps and valves are controlled by an electronic control unit.

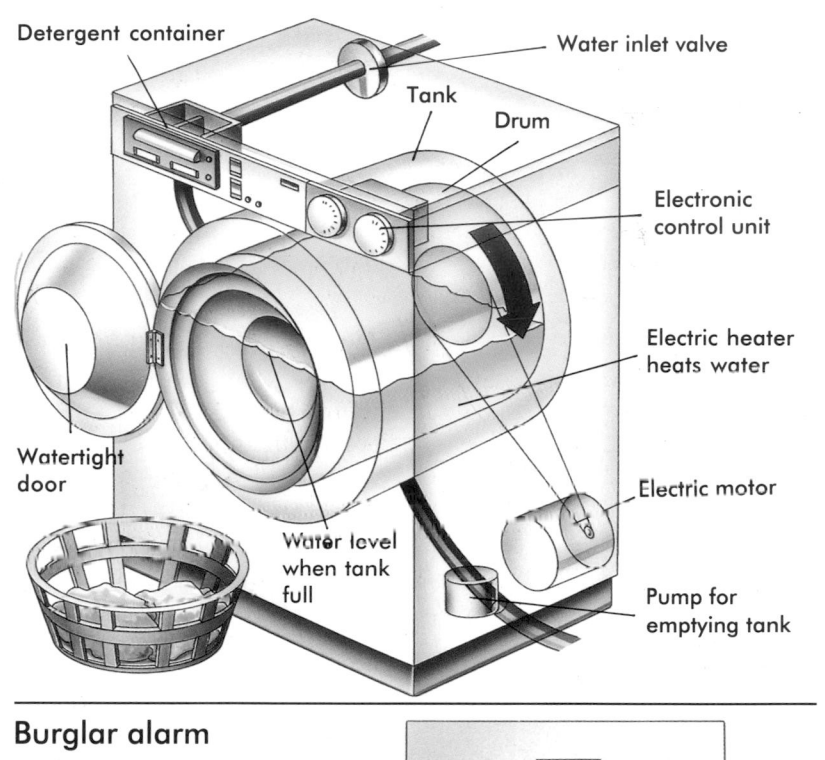

Detergent container

Water inlet valve

Tank

Drum

Electronic control unit

Electric heater heats water

Watertight door

Water level when tank full

Electric motor

Pump for emptying tank

Burglar alarm

A burglar alarm uses various kinds of sensors to detect opening doors, breaking windows and movement inside rooms. The sensors and the control panel set off the alarm if any of the sensors are triggered.

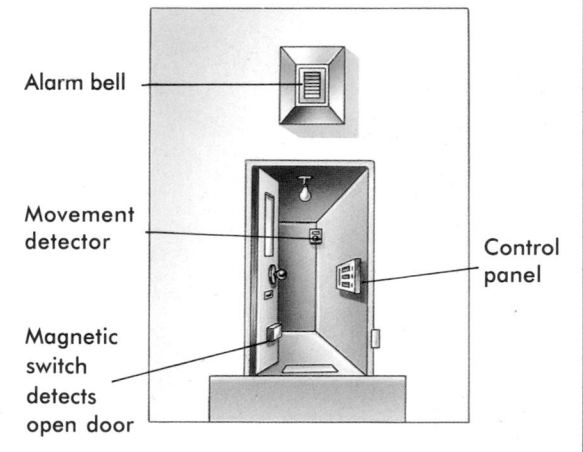

Alarm bell

Movement detector

Control panel

Magnetic switch detects open door

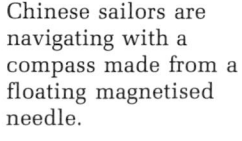

AD 1100

Chinese sailors are navigating with a compass made from a floating magnetised needle.

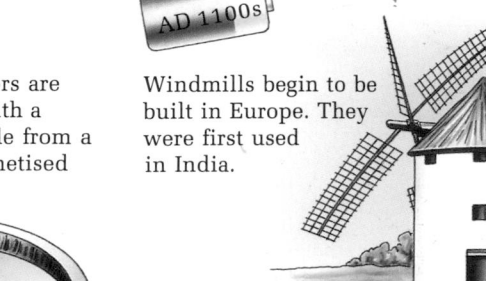

AD 1100s

Windmills begin to be built in Europe. They were first used in India.

AD 1200s

The sternpost rudder is used in Northern Europe. Before this, oars are used for steering.

From AD 1200

Full rigging is used on ships. Full rigging is a mixture of square and triangular sails.

Making music

All musical instruments make sound by making vibrations in the air. Different types of instruments do this in different ways, which is why they have their own individual sounds.

About sound

Sound is made by vibrating air. The air gets squeezed together in some places and pulled apart in others to make vibrations. These vibrations travel through the air. Your ears detect the vibrations so that you can hear the sounds.

Air pulled apart

Air squeezed together

Electric guitar

An electric guitar is played in a similar way to an acoustic guitar, but the sound is made differently. Under each string is a coil of wire called a pick-up. The vibrating string causes an electrical signal in the pick-up, which makes a loudspeaker vibrate.

Pick-up   Steel string

Coil of wire

Plucking strings

A guitar is played by plucking its strings. This makes the strings vibrate, which in turn makes the air around them vibrate. Putting a finger on a string makes the part that vibrates shorter in length. This makes the string vibrate faster, making a higher note.

Strings

Fingers on fretboard shorten strings

Strings plucked or strummed here

Violin

Like a guitar, a violin makes its sound with vibrating strings. A bow string is made of hairs gathered together. The ripples on the hairs makes one of the violin strings vibrate as the violinist pulls the bow across it.

Bow

String

Bow string

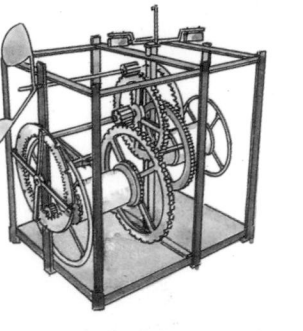

AD 1300s

The first mechanical clocks are built in Europe.

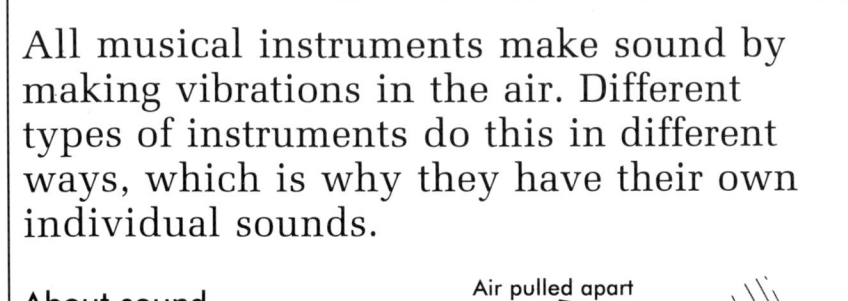

AD 1400s

Spectacles begin to be used in China and Italy.

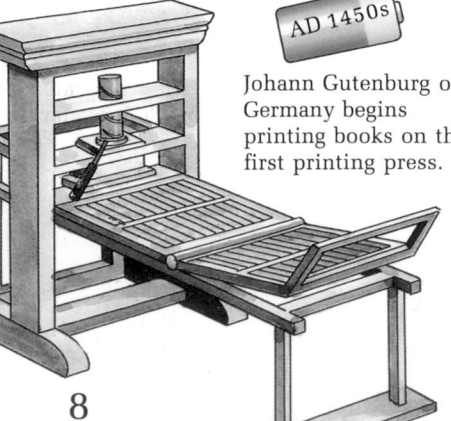

AD 1450s

Johann Gutenburg of Germany begins printing books on the first printing press.

AD 1452

Leonardo da Vinci, one of the greatest inventors and artists in history, is born in Italy.

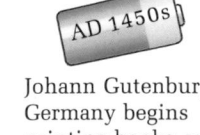

INTERNET LINK http://www.edisonkids.com/heroxb/main.htm
Learn all about energy at this Californian website, where you can play the
Safety Race Game and read about cool electric cars!

Flute

A flute is a metal tube with a hole at one
end. Blowing across the hole makes the
air inside the tube vibrate, making sound.
Along the side of the flute are more holes
which can be opened and closed,
changing the note that the flute makes.

Blowing here makes the air vibrate

Holes to change note

Keys held down
with fingers

Vibrating reeds

Some instruments,
such as the
clarinet, contain a
reed. Blowing into
the mouthpiece
makes the reed
vibrate. This makes
the air inside the
body of the
instrument vibrate,
making sound.

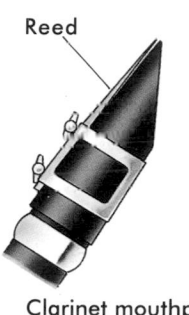

Reed

Clarinet mouthpiece

Skin

Sound wave

Drums

The tight skin of a drum moves down
and up when it is hit with a drum stick.
This produces big vibrations in the air,
which make the drum's booming sound.

Synthesising sounds

A synthesiser (or electronic keyboard)
makes sounds using electronics. Pressing
a key makes an electrical signal which is
played through a speaker. The signals
can be made to sound like a wide range
of real instruments.

Buttons to select
different sounds

Keyboard

Sampling sounds

Some of the latest synthesisers can
make almost any sorts of sounds.
They do it by recording the sound
and storing it. This is called a
sample. The sound can then be
played on the keyboard of
the synthesiser.

Sampled sounds can
be loaded into a
computer and altered

Sampled sound

Synthesiser with built-in sampler

AD 1500s

The spinning wheel,
used to spin wool
fibres, is in use all
over Europe.

cAD 1500

The first watch is
made by Peter Henlein
of Germany. It uses a
wound-up spring for
power.

AD 1590

The compound microscope
(one with more than one
lens) is made in Holland.

AD 1608

Hans Lippershey of
Holland builds what
may have been the
first telescope.

Clocks and watches

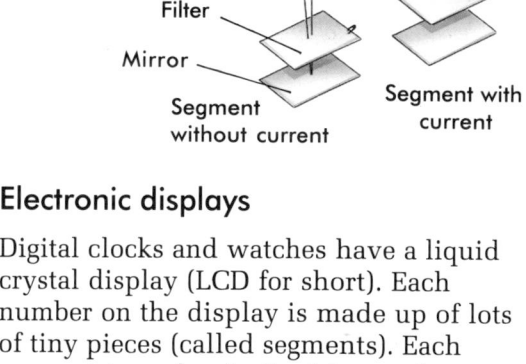

Clocks and watches measure time going by and show what hour of the day it is. Imagine a day without knowing the time!

Keeping track of time

Clocks and watches keep track of time by counting how many times a regular thing happens. For example, a complete swing of a pendulum always takes the same time. A pendulum clock uses this to keep going at the right speed.

Escapement
Spring
Balance wheel

Event happens at regular intervals

Mechanism works out number of seconds or minutes

Hands or electronic display shows time

Turning hands

The hands of a clock or watch are there to show the time. The hour and minute hands must move very slowly, and at different speeds. The speeds are controlled by a set of gears that links the hands together.

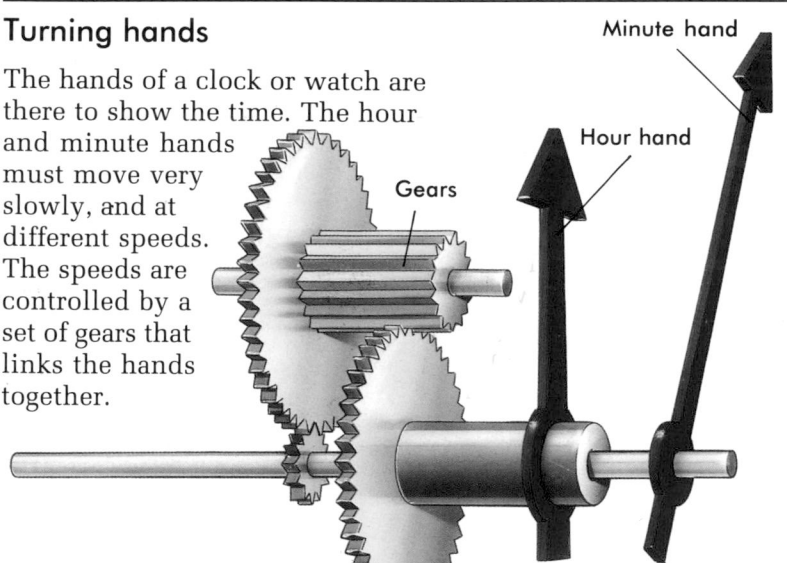

Minute hand

Hour hand

Gears

Balancing springs

Small clocks and watches that don't use electronics are controlled by a balance spring. This is a small wheel that is turned one way then the other by a spring. It's a bit like a pendulum, and it controls the clock in the same way.

Crystal
Filter
Mirror
Segment without current
Segment with current

Electronic displays

Digital clocks and watches have a liquid crystal display (LCD for short). Each number on the display is made up of lots of tiny pieces (called segments). Each segment is made of a liquid crystal. Normally, the crystals look light. But if a tiny electric current is passed through a crystal, it makes it look black.

AD 1620s

The first recorded submarine dive is made by Dutchman Cornelius Drebbel. The wood and leather craft has twelve oarsmen.

AD 1642

Frenchman Blaise Pascal makes a mechanical adding machine.

AD 1656

The first clock controlled by a pendulum is patented by Christiaan Huygens of Holland.

AD 1668

English scientist Isaac Newton invents the reflecting telescope.

INTERNET LINK http://www.howstuffworks.com/digital-clock.htm
Find out more about the making of digital clocks from the experts at 'How Stuff Works' – the web's top science site for kids only!

Quartz timing

Most modern clocks and watches are controlled by a tiny crystal of quartz. When a battery is connected to the crystal, the crystal vibrates, giving out a tiny electrical signal. It vibrates thousands of times a second, always at the same rate. Electronics count the number of vibrations and control the hands (with an electric motor) or an LCD display. Quartz clocks are very accurate. They only gain or lose about one thousandth of a second in a day.

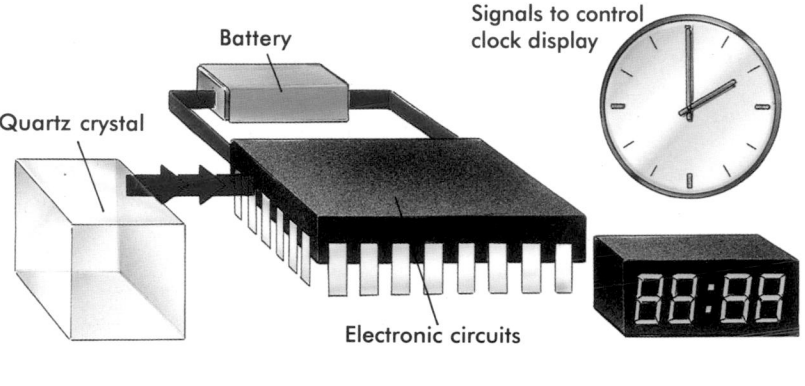

Battery

Signals to control clock display

Quartz crystal

Electronic circuits

Swinging timer

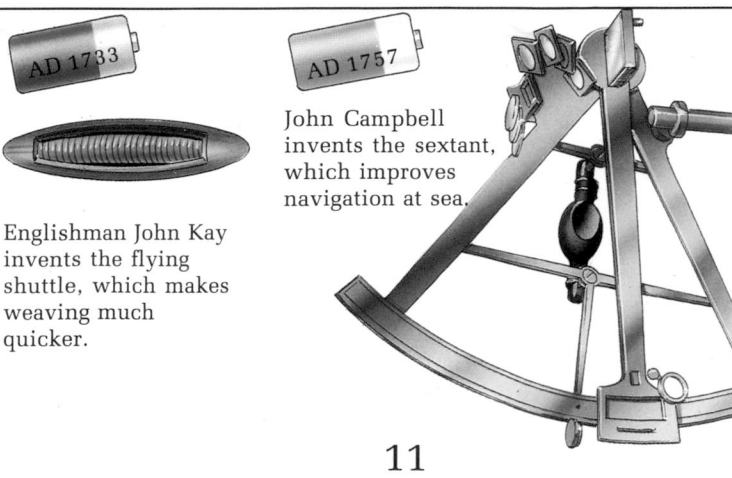

Escapement

Wheel clicks round as pendulum swings

Pendulum

Some old-style clocks are controlled by a swinging pendulum. Each swing of the pendulum takes the same time, and each swing allows a wheel to turn by one tooth. This mechanism is called an escapement. Gear wheels make sure that the minute and hour hands turn at the right speed.

Alarming clocks

An alarm clock waits until a set time and then sounds its alarm. Mechanical alarm clocks have a mechanism which releases the bell hammer when the hour hand moves past the alarm hand. In an electronic alarm clock, electronic circuits check the alarm time against the actual time at the beginning of each minute.

Clock power

A clock needs power to keep it going. Mechanical clocks have a spring which unwinds gradually to keep the clock going. Other clocks are powered by a falling weight. Electronic clocks use battery or mains power.

Spring

Wound-up spring

Auto winding

Some watches wind up automatically. Inside is a weight which swings about as you move your arm during the day. This movement winds the watch spring through a system of gears.

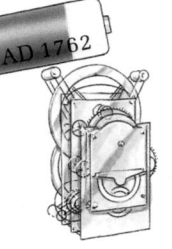

Weight

Watch

AD 1712
Thomas Newcomen of England builds his first steam engine, used for pumping.

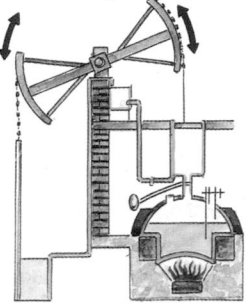

AD 1733
Englishman John Kay invents the flying shuttle, which makes weaving much quicker.

AD 1757
John Campbell invents the sextant, which improves navigation at sea.

AD 1762
Englishman John Harrison is awarded a prize for the first successful marine chronometer.

Engines and gears

Cars, motorbikes, trucks and trains all have engines. The engines turn the energy in fuel (such as petrol) into power to make the vehicle move.

Internal combustion

Most vehicle engines are internal combustion engines. This means that fuel burns inside the engine, pushing pistons to make a shaft turn. Car engines normally have four or six pistons.

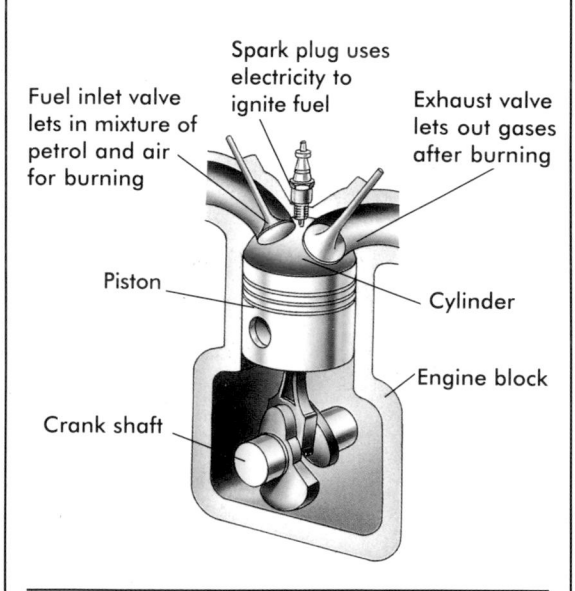

Spark plug uses electricity to ignite fuel

Fuel inlet valve lets in mixture of petrol and air for burning

Exhaust valve lets out gases after burning

Piston

Cylinder

Engine block

Crank shaft

Turbo power

A turbo-charger increases the power of an engine by forcing extra air and fuel into the cylinders. The turbo is a pump that is turned by the exhaust gases rushing out of the cylinders.

Four-stroke cycle

Each piston in an engine moves up and down continuously in a cycle. In each cycle, fuel is put into the cylinder and burned, and the waste gases are expelled. Most engines use a four-stroke cycle, which means that the piston moves up and down twice in each cycle.

1 Induction stroke

Inlet valve open

Piston moves down

Fuel and air are sucked into cylinder

2 Compression stroke

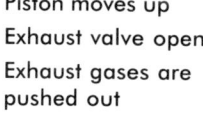

Valves closed

Piston moves up

Fuel and air are squeezed

3 Ignition stroke

Valves closed

Spark plug makes a spark

Fuel and air explodes

Piston is pushed down

4 Exhaust stroke

Piston moves up

Exhaust valve open

Exhaust gases are pushed out

Timing it right

As each cylinder goes through its cycle, controls make sure that the valves open and close at the right time and that the spark plugs make their sparks at the right time. A camshaft controls the valves. The ignition system controls the spark plugs.

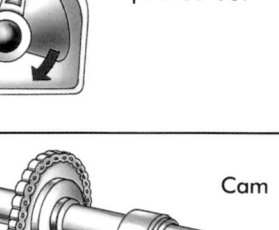

Cam

Camshaft is turned by a chain attached to the crank shaft

Valve open

Valve closed

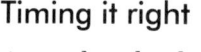

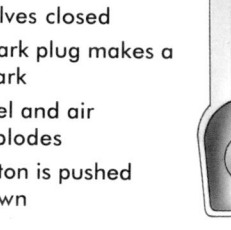
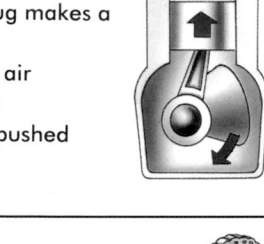
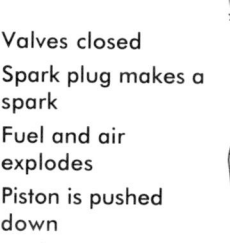
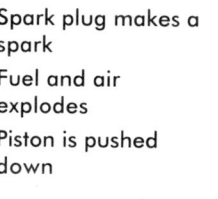
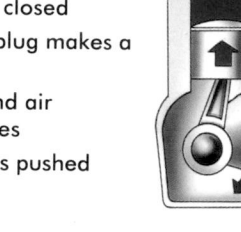

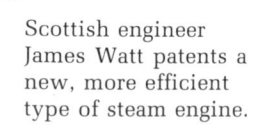

AD 1769

Scottish engineer James Watt patents a new, more efficient type of steam engine.

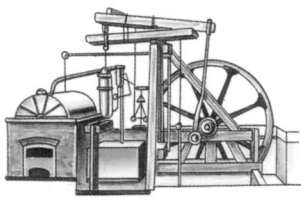

AD 1769

Nicolas Cugnot, a French army engineer, builds the first steam vehicle.

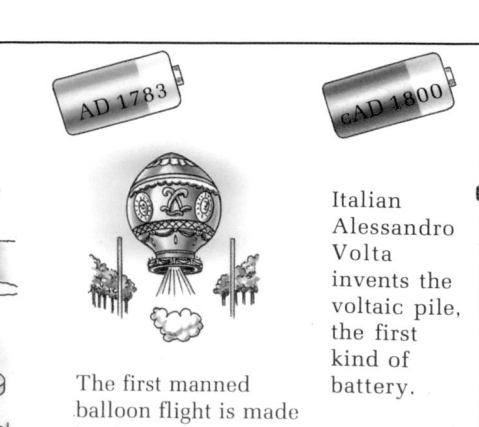

AD 1783

The first manned balloon flight is made by the Montgolfier brothers.

cAD 1800

Italian Alessandro Volta invents the voltaic pile, the first kind of battery.

INTERNET LINK http://www.nationalgeographic.com/features/96/inventions
Click on 'It's Your Turn' and try your hand at inventing with the Inventions Colouring Book.
There are 'wild and wacky' games to play too.

Into gear

On a bicycle (where you are the engine!), the gears make cycling uphill easier and mean you can pedal at a comfortable speed on the flat. The less the wheels turn for each turn of the pedals, the easier it is to pedal.

Rear gear wheels

Pedals

Front gear wheel

High gear — for level ground

Low gear — for starting off and steep hills

The gear box of a car is more complicated than the gears on a bicycle, but it does the same job. It lets the car start and stop, and it means that the the car can travel fast without the engine turning too fast.

Clutch control

The engine is connected to the gearbox by a clutch. Pressing the clutch pedal disconnects the engine from the gearbox and the wheels. The clutch is used for starting the car from a standstill and for changing gears.

Clutch plates

Shaft from engine

Shaft to gearbox

Pressing pedal separates the plates

Diesel engine

A diesel engine works very much like a petrol engine. The difference is that it has no spark plugs. When the fuel and air mixture is squeezed by the piston, it gets very hot, making the fuel ignite.

Engines on rails

Diesel locomotive

Diesel engine

Shafts to drive wheels round

Diesel electric locomotive

Diesel engine

Generator

Electric motors

Pantograph collects electricity

Electric locomotive

Electric motors

Modern locomotives have three main types of engine. Electric locomotives have electric motors. The electric current comes from overhead cables or the rails. Diesel locomotives have a powerful diesel engine. Diesel-electric locomotives have a diesel engine which turns a generator to produce electricity for electric motors.

AD 1802

A successful steamboat, the *Charlotte Dundas*, is launched by William Symington.

AD 1804

Railway history is made as Englishman Richard Trevithick builds the world's first steam locomotive.

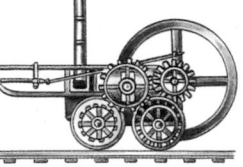

AD 1814

Gas street lighting is introduced in the district of Westminster in London.

AD 1818

Engineer Marc Isambard Brunel designs a tunnelling machine for digging under the River Thames in London.

Vehicle safety and security

Just as important as its engine are the things that make a vehicle safe. These include brakes, safety belts and road signals.

Bicycle brakes

Applying bicycle brakes pushes rubber brake blocks against the rim of the wheel. The friction between the block and the rim tries to stop the wheel turning, and so slows the bicycle. The brake handle is a lever, which makes it easy to brake hard with a fairly light squeeze.

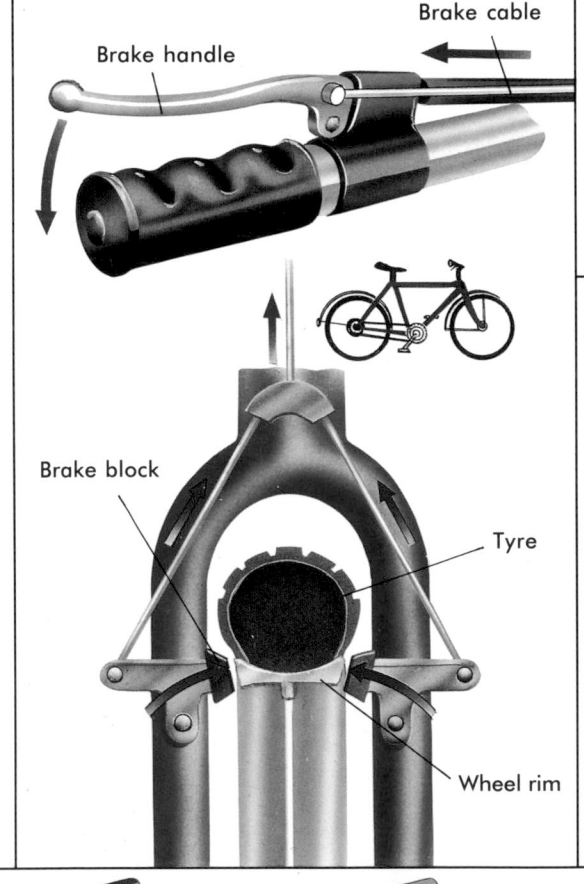

Brake cable

Brake handle

Brake block

Tyre

Wheel rim

Discs and drums

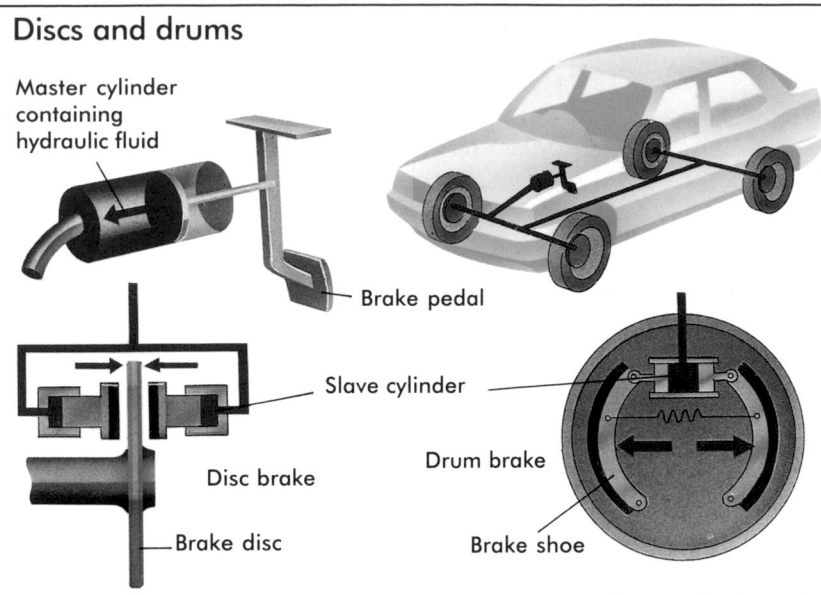

Master cylinder containing hydraulic fluid

Brake pedal

Slave cylinder

Disc brake

Drum brake

Brake disc

Brake shoe

Discs and drums are the two types of brake used on vehicles. Disc brakes are similar to bicycle brakes, but much more powerful. Brake pads press against a disc attached to the wheel, slowing it down. In drum brakes, brake shoes press on the inside of a drum attached to the wheel. Most car brakes use hydraulics (the process of transferring a force through a liquid) so that a light press on the brake pedal provides strong braking.

Belt up

A seat belt is wound round a drum that turns. Pulling the belt gently makes the drum rotate slowly, paying out the belt. But a sharp pull makes the drum rotate very quickly. This makes arms fly out, stopping the drum turning and holding the belt.

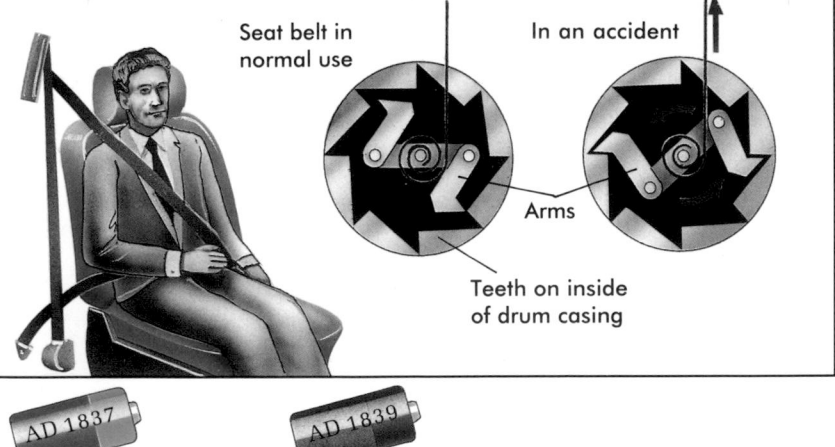

Seat belt in normal use

In an accident

Arms

Teeth on inside of drum casing

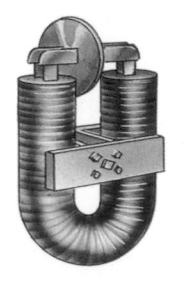

AD 1831

English scientist Michael Faraday discovers the principle of the electric motor.

AD 1834

Charles Babbage devises a mechanical computer called an analytical engine. But it is too complex to build.

AD 1837

Samuel Morse invents the system of sending messages on a telegraph as a series of long and short pulses.

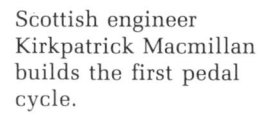

AD 1839

Scottish engineer Kirkpatrick Macmillan builds the first pedal cycle.

Auto locking

Door locks

Receiver

Remote control

A car with electronic locking is locked and unlocked with an electronic key. Like a small television remote control, this sends a coded signal to a receiver inside the car. If the code matches the code stored in the receiver, the doors unlock automatically.

Reflecting roads

Reflectors mark the way on roads that are not lit at night. The specially-shaped glass (often called a prism cat's eye) collects the light from car headlights and reflects it back to where it came from. This makes the reflector look like a tiny light. The reflectors are cleaned automatically when tyres go over them.

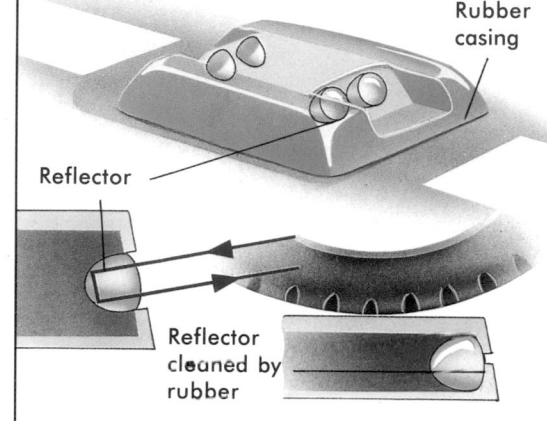

Rubber casing

Reflector

Reflector cleaned by rubber

Air bags

An air bag is like a huge balloon that protects a driver in a crash. If the car stops violently, a detector notes this and activates the air bag, which inflates very quickly, filling the space between the driver and the dashboard.

Air bag

Anti-lock brakes

Braking too hard can make a car's wheels stop turning suddenly (called locking-up). This makes the car skid. An anti-lock braking system (ABS for short) uses computers to sense if the brakes are about to lock. If they are, it releases the brakes slightly.

Catalytic conversion

A catalytic converter removes most of the dangerous chemicals from vehicle exhaust fumes. The catalytic converter is part of the exhaust pipe. Chemicals in a filter make the dangerous chemicals less harmful before they go into the atmosphere.

Exhaust to air

Layers of chemicals

Exhaust from engine

Stop and go

Modern traffic signals decide when to change to allow vehicles to flow across a junction. Under the road is a loop of wire which makes a weak magnetic field. When a car stops at the line it changes the magnetic field. The control box changes the lights if no cars are crossing in the other direction.

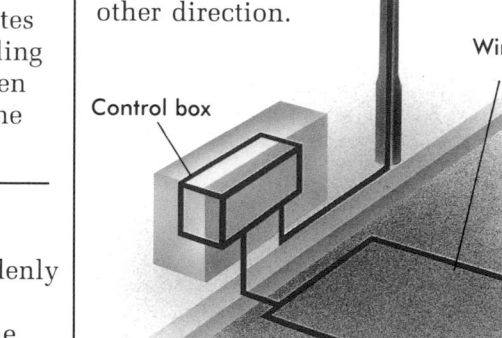

Lights

Control box

Wire loop

Englishman William Fox Talbot invents the negative-positive method of photography.

AD 1847

Thomas Edison, who patented more than a thousand inventions, is born in the USA.

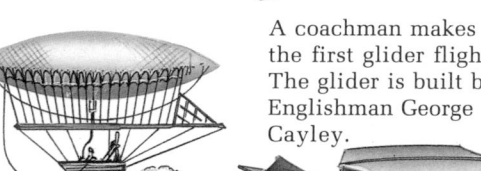

AD 1852

The first airship takes to the air, piloted by French engineer Henri Giffard.

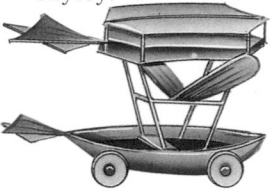

AD 1853

A coachman makes the first glider flight. The glider is built by Englishman George Cayley.

Flying machines

There are many different kinds of aircraft. Most aircraft, such as large airliners and small sports planes, have wings to keep them up. Other types, such as helicopters and hot-air balloons, have different ways of flying.

Wings

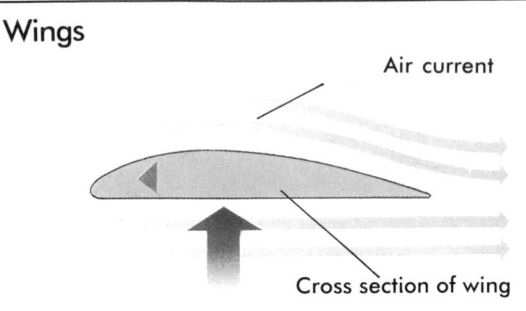

Air current

Cross section of wing

Wings keep an aircraft in the air. The special shape of the wing is called an aerofoil. It makes the air on top of the wing go faster than underneath. This sucks the wing upwards. The suck is called lift. The aircraft must be moving very fast for the wings to work.

How to fly

Special parts of an aircraft make it fly straight, turn, climb or descend. There are three main controls: the rudder, ailerons and elevators. They are called control surfaces.

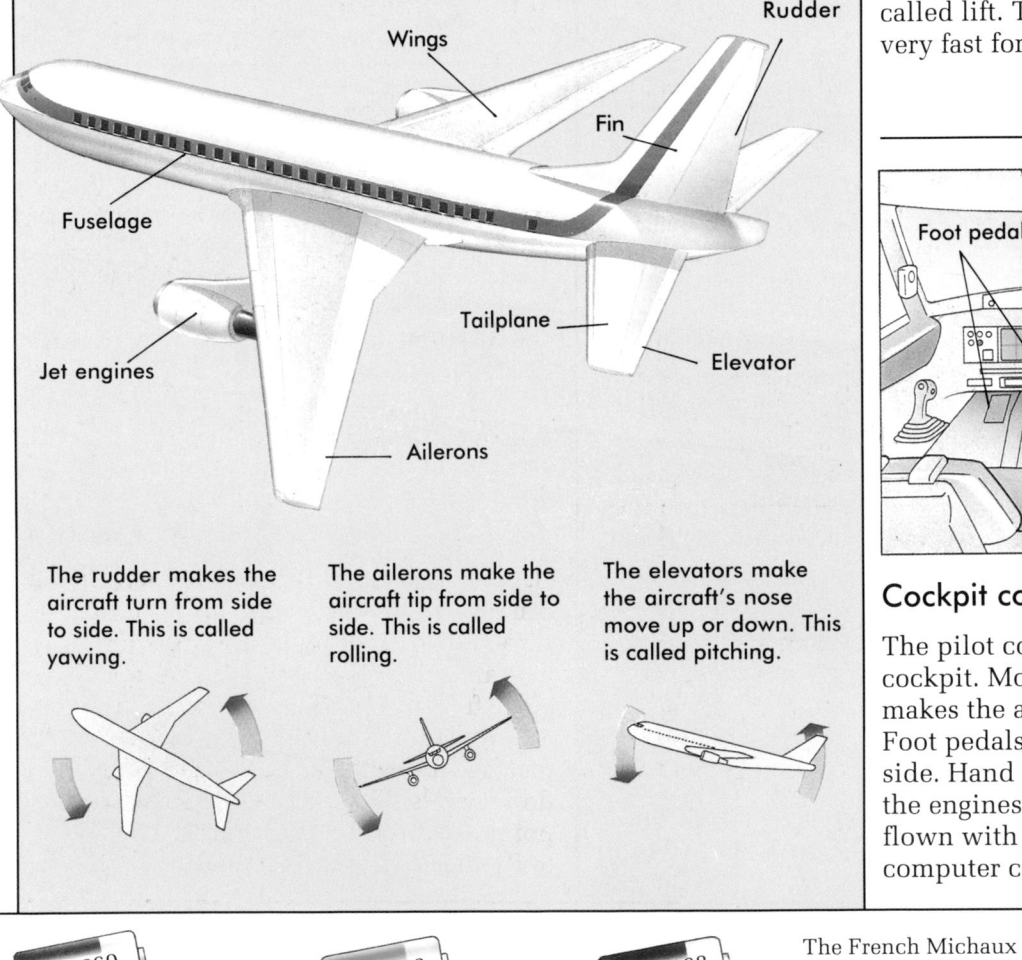

Rudder

Wings

Fin

Fuselage

Tailplane

Jet engines

Elevator

Ailerons

The rudder makes the aircraft turn from side to side. This is called yawing.

The ailerons make the aircraft tip from side to side. This is called rolling.

The elevators make the aircraft's nose move up or down. This is called pitching.

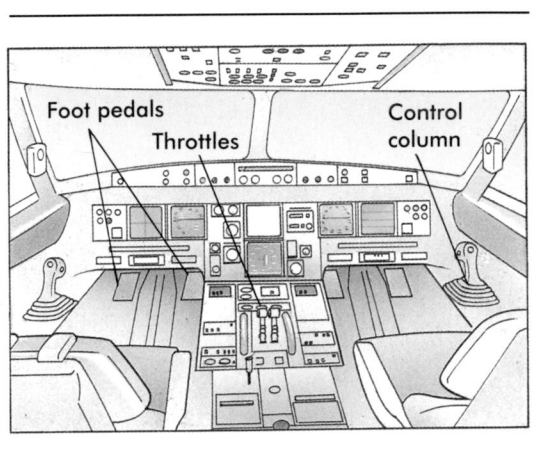

Foot pedals

Throttles

Control column

Cockpit controls

The pilot controls the aeroplane from the cockpit. Moving the control column makes the ailerons and elevators move. Foot pedals move the rudder from side to side. Hand throttles change the power of the engines. Some modern airliners are flown with the help of a computer. The computer can even land the aircraft.

AD 1860

Étienne Lenior of France builds the first successful internal combustion engine. It uses gas as a fuel.

AD 1863

A small clinical thermometer is invented. Doctors use it to take their patients' temperature.

AD 1868

The French Michaux brothers build the first motorcycle. It has a steam engine under the saddle.

AD 1876

Alexander Graham Bell invents the telephone.

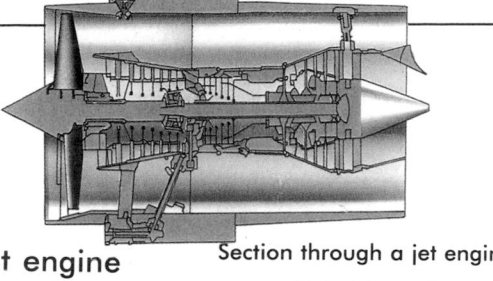

Jet engine

Section through a jet engine

Jet engines are very powerful. Aircraft that need to fly fast, such as fighter planes and airliners, use them. Air is sucked into the engine and is mixed with fuel. This mixture burns, sending a very fast stream of hot gases out of the back. This pushes the aircraft forwards.

Helicopter

Instead of having wings fixed to a fuselage (body), a helicopter has wings called rotor blades attached to a rotor. The rotor spins round very fast to make lift. This lets it take off and land vertically. To move forwards, backwards and sideways, the pilot tilts the rotor. The tail rotor stops the fuselage spinning round in the opposite direction to the rotor.

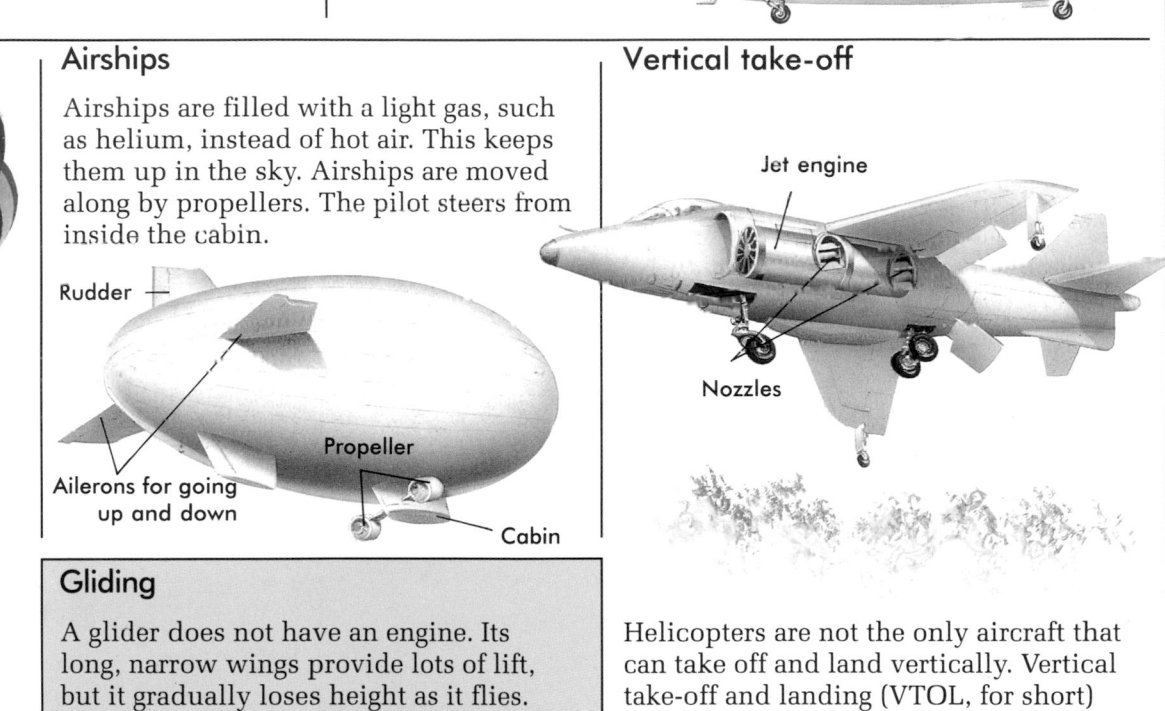

Rotor blade   Main rotor

Engine

Tail rotor

Airships

Airships are filled with a light gas, such as helium, instead of hot air. This keeps them up in the sky. Airships are moved along by propellers. The pilot steers from inside the cabin.

Rudder

Ailerons for going up and down

Propeller

Cabin

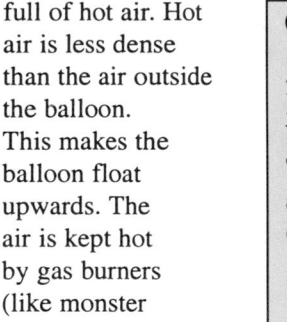

Hot-air fliers

Hot air balloons stay in the air because they are full of hot air. Hot air is less dense than the air outside the balloon. This makes the balloon float upwards. The air is kept hot by gas burners (like monster camping stoves) above the basket.

Vertical take-off

Jet engine

Nozzles

Gliding

A glider does not have an engine. Its long, narrow wings provide lots of lift, but it gradually loses height as it flies. The pilot needs to find places where the air is rising, called thermals. Thermals are often found above warm areas of land.

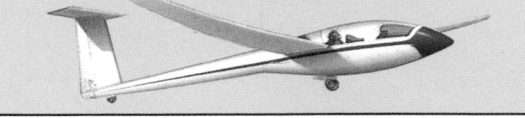

Helicopters are not the only aircraft that can take off and land vertically. Vertical take-off and landing (VTOL, for short) aircraft can do the same. The stream of gases from the jet engines comes out through nozzles on the sides of the fuselage. For take-off the nozzles point downwards. Then they slowly swivel to point backwards and the aircraft begins to fly like a normal jet plane.

AD 1877

Thomas Edison builds his phonograph, which is the first machine to record and play sound.

AD 1879

Thomas Edison makes an electric light bulb that lasts for 13.5 hours.

AD 1879

A train powered by an electric motor runs for the first time. It is built by Werner von Siemens of Germany.

Ships and boats

Ships and boats have been used for thousands of years for moving people and goods. Most ships and boats are quite simple, but there are some more complicated types, such as hovercraft and hydrofoils.

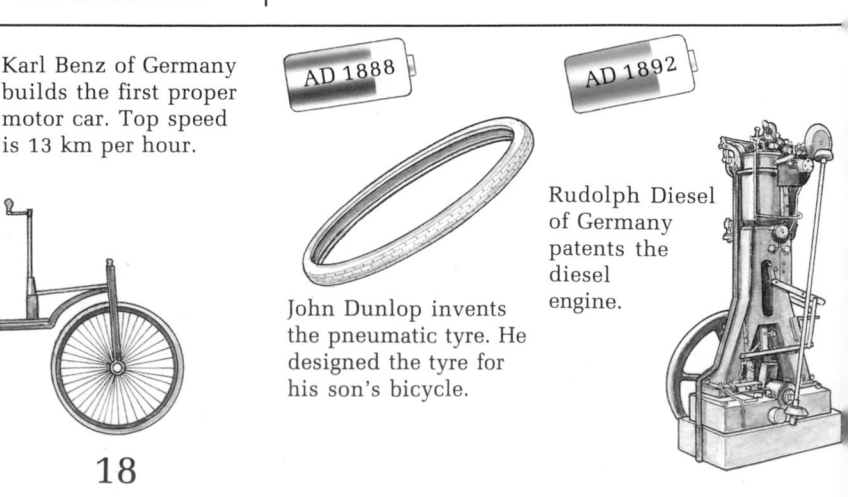

Propeller

Hull   Engine   Shaft   Propeller   Rudder

Steering

Ships and boats are steered by rudders. The rudder dips into the water at the back of the hull. When the ship is moving through the water, turning the rudder to the side makes it push on the water flowing past. The water pushes back, making the back of the ship move sideways. This is how the boat turns.

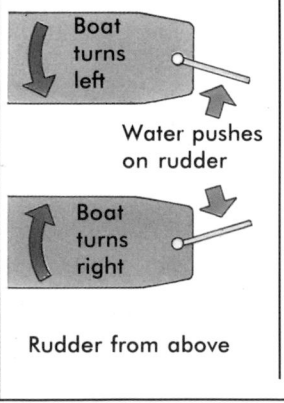

Boat turns left

Water pushes on rudder

Boat turns right

Rudder from above

Full steam ahead

Most ships and boats are pushed along by propellers. The propeller is found under the water at the back of the hull. It spins round, pushing against the water. Large cargo ships have propellers measuring several metres across.

Most ships and boats have diesel engines for turning their propellers. The engine is in an engine room inside the hull. It turns a long shaft which is connected to the propeller.

Sonar

Modern ships use sonar to find out how deep the water is. Sonar stands for SOund Navigation And Ranging. The sonar equipment sends out a pinging noise. The sound bounces off the bottom of the sea and the sonar listens for its echo. The deeper the water, the longer the signal takes to travel to the seabed and back.

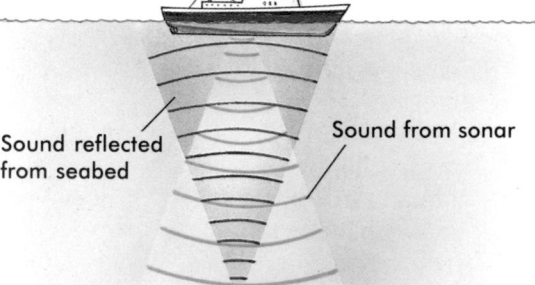

Sound reflected from seabed

Sound from sonar

Radar

Radar screen

Radar dish

Radar stands for RAdio Detection And Range finding. It is a navigation aid used by ships to locate other ships and the shore in bad weather. The radar equipment sends out a beam of radio waves. The waves bounce off any objects they hit and back to the radar. The objects appear on a screen.

AD 1885

Gottlieb Daimler of Germany tests a petrol engine on a motorcycle.

AD 1885

Karl Benz of Germany builds the first proper motor car. Top speed is 13 km per hour.

AD 1888

John Dunlop invents the pneumatic tyre. He designed the tyre for his son's bicycle.

AD 1892

Rudolph Diesel of Germany patents the diesel engine.

Sailing boats

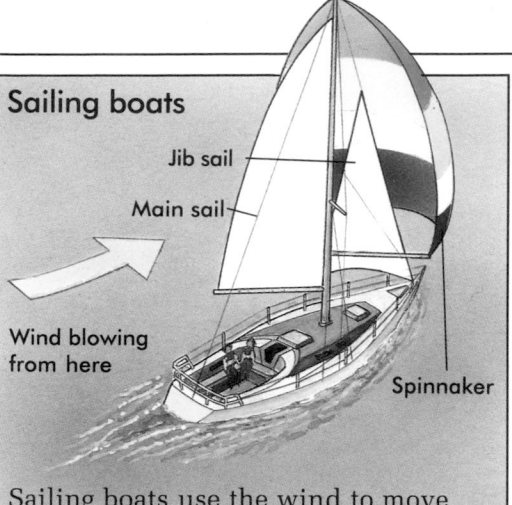

Jib sail

Main sail

Wind blowing from here

Spinnaker

Sailing boats use the wind to move along. The sails are fixed to a mast. Using ropes, the crew can change the angle of the sails to make the best use of the wind. Underneath the boat is a keel to stop the boat drifting sideways.

Under the sea

A submarine can travel on the surface of the sea and below it. It dives and surfaces by filling and emptying its ballast tanks, which makes it heavier or lighter. When it is submerged the submarine moves up and down using rudder-like hydroplanes.

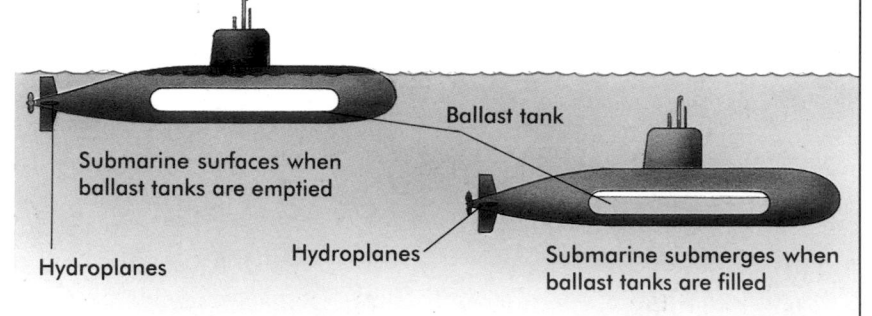

Ballast tank

Submarine surfaces when ballast tanks are emptied

Hydroplanes

Hydroplanes

Submarine submerges when ballast tanks are filled

Diesel engines use up air and make poisonous fumes, which makes them dangerous in a submerged submarine. So a submarine uses a diesel engine on the surface and an electric motor when it is submerged. Nuclear-powered submarines can stay submerged for many months.

Navigating from space

The latest system for navigation is the global positioning system (GPS, for short). A GPS receiver collects signals from satellites around the Earth. It then works out its position on the Earth to within about 20 metres.

A GPS receiver

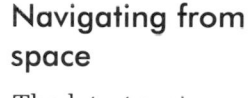

Hovercraft

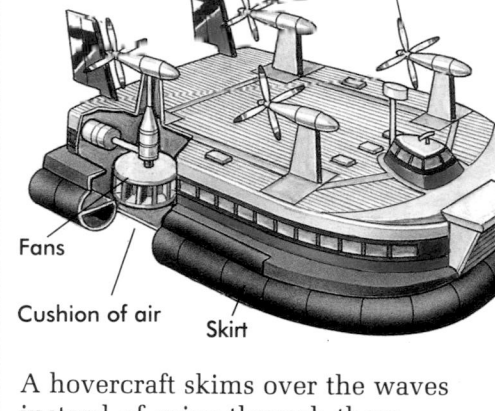

Propellers push craft along

Fans

Cushion of air

Skirt

A hovercraft skims over the waves instead of going through them. Skimming means that a hovercraft can go much faster than a normal boat. Around the bottom of a hovercraft is a rubber 'skirt' which contains a cushion of air on which the hovercraft sits. Large fans blow air into the cushion to keep it inflated.

Hydrofoil

A hydrofoil flies through the water on foils. The foils are like an aircraft's wings. At slow speed a hydrofoil's hull is in the water. As it speeds up, the foils start to work, and the hull rises above the water. Because only the foils touch the water, the craft can go very fast.

Hydrofoil

Foils

AD 1893

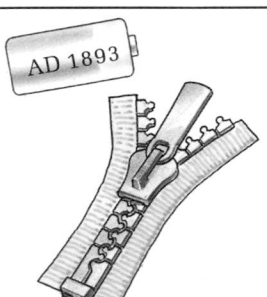

The zip fastener is invented by Whitcomb Judson of the USA.

AD 1894

Thomas Edison demonstrates a machine that he calls the kinetoscope. It shows moving pictures.

AD 1895

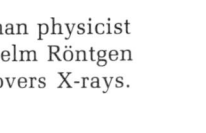

German physicist Wilhelm Röntgen discovers X-rays.

AD 1898

Guglielmo Marconi of Italy succeeds in sending radio signals about 100 kilometres.

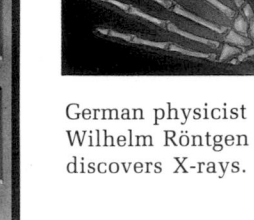

Computers

Computers seem to be everywhere in our lives today. We use computers at home, school and work, and play games on computer game consoles. There are also small computer-like devices inside many domestic appliances, such as washing machines and televisions.

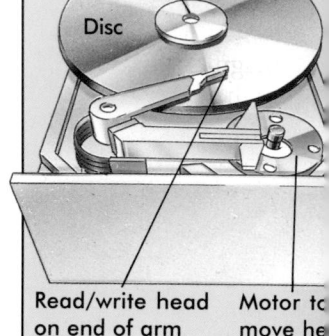

Motor to turn disc

Disc

Read/write head on end of arm

Motor to move he[ad]

Hardware

The parts of a computer itself — the electronic bits and pieces such as microchips, electronic circuits, keyboard and monitor — are called hardware. Although hardware is extremely complicated, it can only do quite simple things. The words and pictures (the data) that you see on a computer's monitor are all stored inside the computer as 1s and 0s. The computer 'processes' the data — moving it from one place to another, or adding it together.

Software

A computer is useless if it's not told what to do. It needs a computer program. A program is a list of instructions which tells the computer what to do with the data. The program and the numbers it uses are called software.

The memory is where all the programs and data are stored.

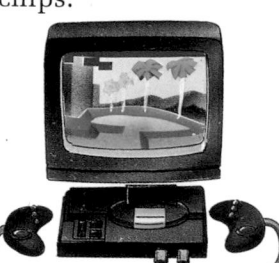

Computer games

Computer game consoles are computers specialised for showing animated pictures and making sounds. Plug-in game cartridges contain software contained on ROM memory chips.

Data gets out of the computer through outputs. It goes to output devices, such as printers or plotters. Outputs are also used to control machines, such as manufacturing tools.

A portion of RAM is used to store the pictures that appear on the computer's monitor.

'Random access' memory (RAM) is memory that the CPU can send data to and get it back from.

The data in 'read only' memory (ROM) is permanent. It is not lost when the computer is turned off.

The central processing unit (CPU) is the brain of a computer. It does all the calculations and controls the rest of the computer.

Data gets into the computer through inputs. An input can get data from various sources, such as a keyboard or discs.

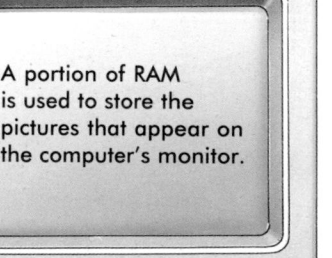

AD 1897

The first boat powered by a steam turbine was built by Englishman Charles Parsons. It breaks all speed records in 1897.

AD 1898

Enrico Forlanini develops a new type of boat — the hydrofoil.

AD 1901

English engineer Hubert Booth invents the vacuum cleaner. A few years later he builds the first small domestic vacuum.

AD 1903

The American Wright brothers make the first flight in a heavier-than-air aircraft.

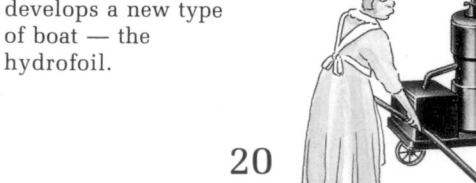

INTERNET LINK http://www.att.com/technology/forfun
Click on 'Brain Spin' to explore the world of the telephone and beyond, from Mr Bell to the Internet.

Disc drive

Inside a disc drive is a flat disc covered in magnetic material which spins round at high speed. The information is 'written' on the disc and 'read' from it by a read/write head. When the disc drive writes, an electromagnet makes a magnetic pattern on the disc. When it reads, it picks up the pattern and electronic circuits turn the pattern back into information.

Floppy disc drives use discs which can be taken out and put in other disc drives. Discs in hard disc drives cannot be removed, but they can hold much more information than a floppy disc. A CD-ROM drive is a cross between a disc drive and a music CD player. CD-ROMs hold huge amounts of information.

Scanner

A scanner turns pictures into a form that a computer can use. It divides the picture into a grid of thousands of tiny dots and works out the shade of each dot. The picture is scanned one row of dots at a time by thousands of tiny light-sensitive devices.

Row of light-sensitive devices

Roller detects scanner moving across picture

Electronic eye

Laser beam

Bar code

Bar codes

The pattern of thick and thin black and white bars on a bar code contains information, such as the price of a product in a supermarket. A bar-code reader scans the bars with a laser beam. It detects widths of the bars and so reads the code.

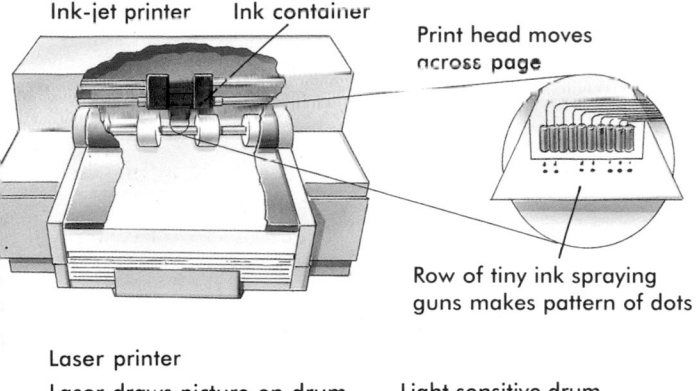

Ink-jet printer   Ink container

Print head moves across page

Row of tiny ink spraying guns makes pattern of dots

Laser printer

Laser draws picture on drum   Light sensitive drum

Drum attracts toner where laser has hit it

Black toner is transferred on to paper

Pins push inked ribbon on to paper to make pattern of dots

Putting it on paper

Printers are used to make a copy of computer information on to paper. There are several different sorts of printer. The main ones are dot-matrix printers, ink-jet printers and laser printers.

Dot-matrix printer head

Mouse

A computer mouse has a rubber ball inside it. When you move the mouse, the ball rolls around and turns two small wheels inside the mouse. Electronic eyes inside the mouse see these wheels move so the computer can move the pointer on the screen.

Wheel to detect forward and backward movement

Rubber ball

Electronic eyes

Wheel to detect side-to-side movement

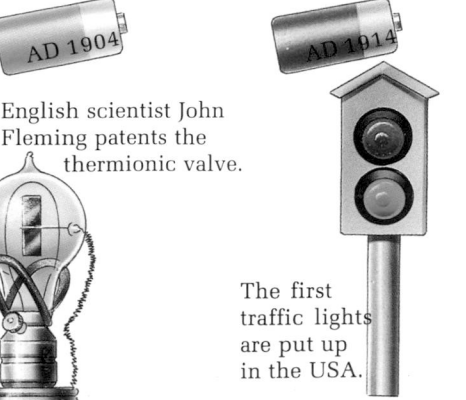

English scientist John Fleming patents the thermionic valve.

The first traffic lights are put up in the USA.

The principle of optic fibres is used to illuminate aircraft instruments.

Scotsman John Logie Baird demonstrates the first television system. The pictures are wobbly and blurred.

AD 1904   AD 1914   AD 1920s   AD 1926

Keeping in touch

Today, we can pick up the telephone and talk to people almost anywhere in the world. We can even make telephone calls from inside our cars and send pictures down the telephone line.

On the telephone

When you talk to a friend on the telephone, your voice is transmitted through a telephone network. It goes from your receiver to the local exchange, down a trunk line (like a telephone motorway) to your friend's local exchange, and then to his or her receiver. If you call somebody in another country, your call might go along an undersea cable or via a satellite in space.

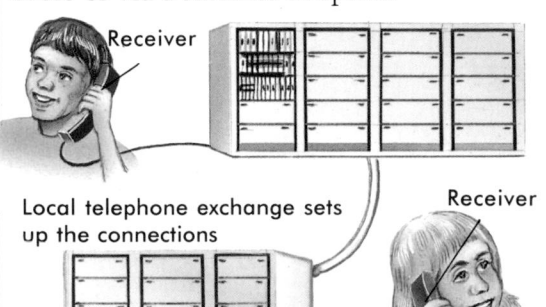

Receiver

Local telephone exchange sets up the connections

Receiver

Inside your receiver

Earpiece

Mouthpiece

The electrical signal goes through a tiny electromagnet. This makes a metal diaphragm vibrate, making sound.

Inside the mouthpiece are thousands of tiny carbon granules. The sound of your voice changes the amount that the granules are pressed together, changing their resistance. This changes the electrical current flowing through the mouthpiece.

The part of a receiver that you talk into is called the mouthpiece. It turns sound into an electric current (called an electrical signal) which changes in strength. The signal can be sent down the telephone line. You listen at the earpiece. It turns electrical signals coming up the telephone line into sound.

Optical fibres

An optical fibre is a thin strand of flexible glass or plastic. When you shine light into one end, it travels along the fibre. The light cannot escape. Instead, it bounces off the inside of the fibre until it arrives at the other end.

Optical fibres are being used instead of wires to carry telephone calls. The electrical signal from your receiver is turned into light signals and sent along the optical fibre. An optical fibre the width of a hair can carry thousands of telephone calls at the same time.

Cladding stops light escaping from fibre

Optical fibre

Light ray

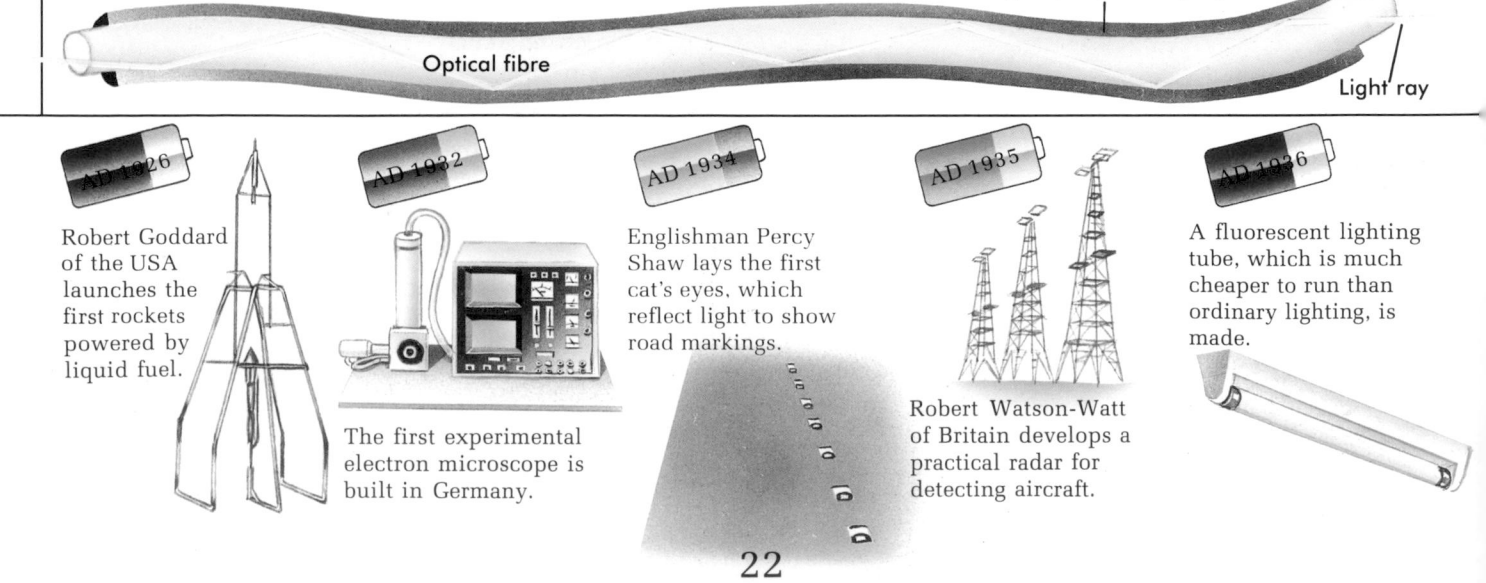

AD 1926 — Robert Goddard of the USA launches the first rockets powered by liquid fuel.

AD 1932 — The first experimental electron microscope is built in Germany.

AD 1934 — Englishman Percy Shaw lays the first cat's eyes, which reflect light to show road markings.

AD 1935 — Robert Watson-Watt of Britain develops a practical radar for detecting aircraft.

AD 1936 — A fluorescent lighting tube, which is much cheaper to run than ordinary lighting, is made.

Making waves

Transmitter

Radio waves

Receiver

Many communication signals travel through the air as invisible radio waves. This is how simple radios, such as walkie-talkies, work. The electrical signal made by the user's voice is turned into radio waves by a radio transmitter. The waves are detected by a radio receiver, turned back into electrical signals and then into sound.

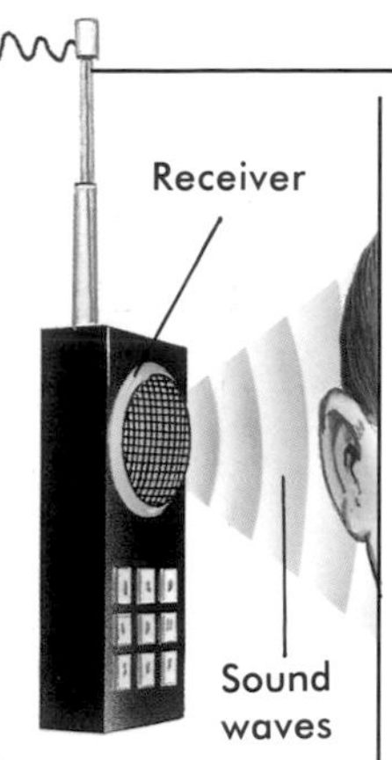

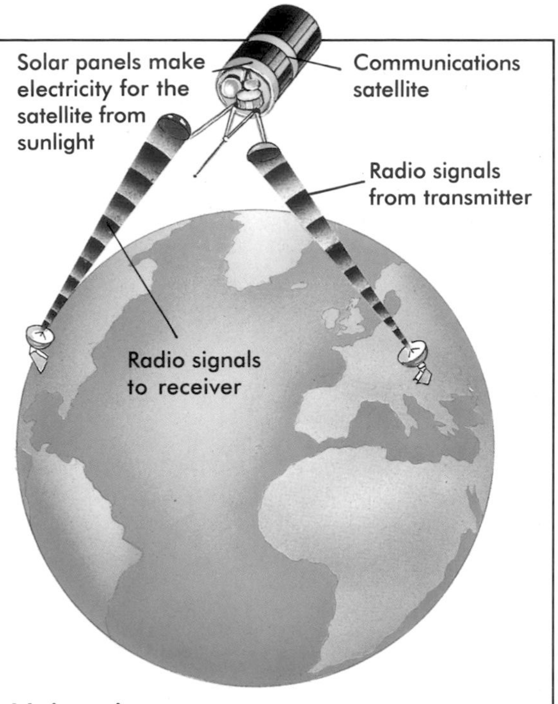

Voice makes sound waves

Sound waves

Solar panels make electricity for the satellite from sunlight

Communications satellite

Radio signals from transmitter

Radio signals to receiver

Mobile chat

Cellular phone

Radio transmitter/receiver

Mobile phone exchange

Local exchange

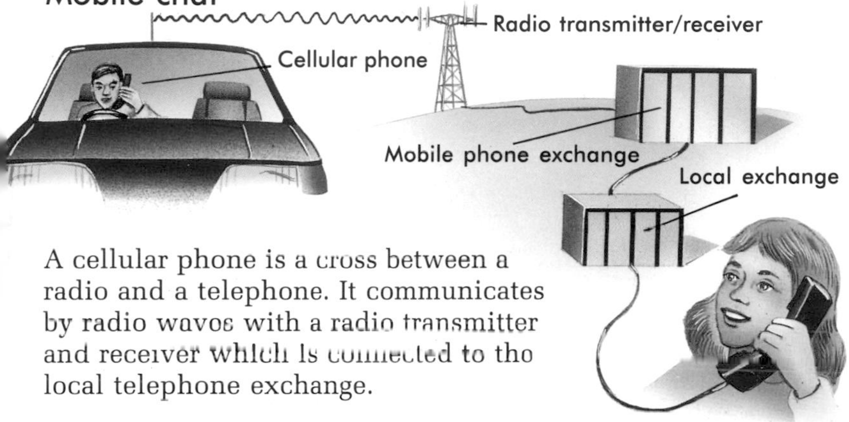

A cellular phone is a cross between a radio and a telephone. It communicates by radio waves with a radio transmitter and receiver which is connected to the local telephone exchange.

Voices in space

Telephone calls between different parts of the world often go via a satellite in orbit around the Earth. The signals are sent to and from the satellite by special radio waves called microwaves.

Fax machines

Picture being sent

Telephone exchange

Paper

Printing device

Row of electronic eyes

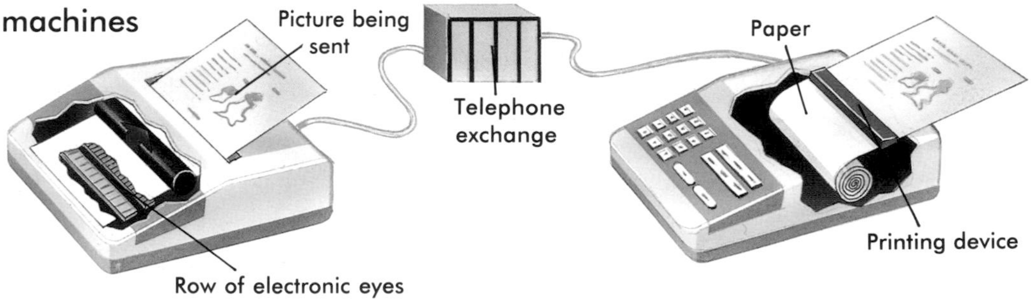

In a fax machine a row of electronic eyes scans the picture, working out which parts are light, and which are dark. It sends the information down the telephone line to the receiving fax machine. The receiving machine prints the dark areas of the picture on to plain paper or special heat-sensitive paper.

Digital signals

Some telephone signals are digitised before they are sent from one exchange to another. This means that the electrical signal is turned into numbers. Digital signals are very clear. There is hardly any noise.

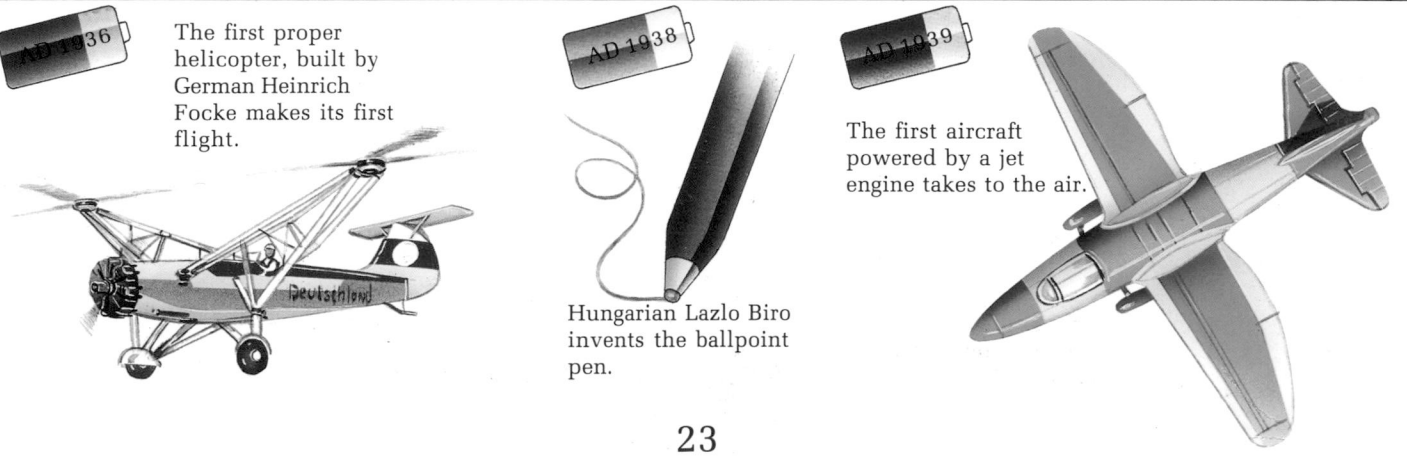

AD 1936 The first proper helicopter, built by German Heinrich Focke makes its first flight.

AD 1938 Hungarian Lazlo Biro invents the ballpoint pen.

AD 1939 The first aircraft powered by a jet engine takes to the air.

Television and radio

Television and radio programmes keep you entertained, tell you about the world, and give you the latest news as it happens. You might take television and radio for granted but imagine what life would be like without them!

Broadcasting

At a broadcasting station, picture and sound information is coded into a wave that can be sent through the atmosphere. The waves are sent out in all directions from a transmitter. Televisions and radios collect the waves and turn them back into pictures or sound.

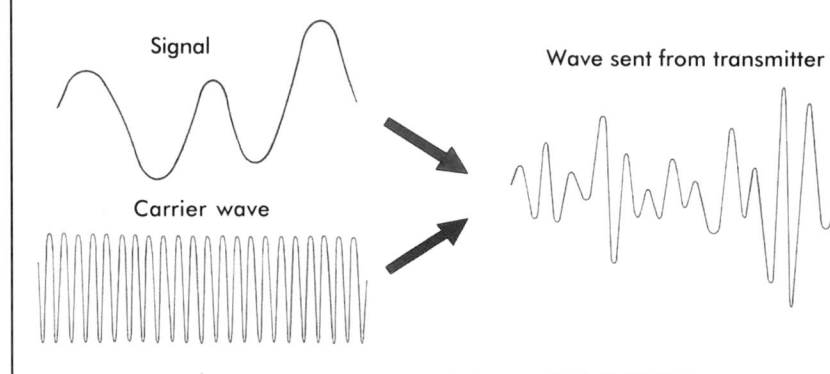

Transmitter · Waves · Aerial · Broadcasting station

What's in a signal?

You can think of radio waves like a row of waves on the sea. The electrical signal from a television camera or microphone is used to change the shape of a wave called the carrier wave. The carrier wave is transmitted.

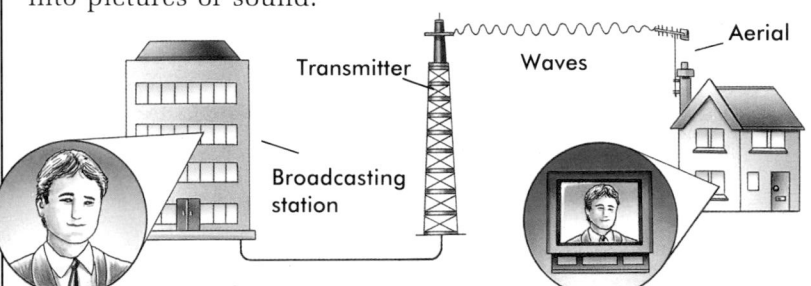

Signal · Carrier wave · Wave sent from transmitter

Television camera

A television camera points at a moving picture and turns it into an electrical signal which can be sent to a television set. This divides the picture into hundreds of rows of dots. Twenty-five times every second it works out the colour and brightness of each dot and makes up a signal. The sound signals are added before the signal is sent to a transmitter for broadcasting.

Tuning in

Signals for different television channels and different radio stations are broadcast using different carrier waves. When you tune your television or radio to a particular programme, you are picking out the waves you want and throwing away all the rest.

Radio

The job of a radio is to collect radio waves, pick out ones from the required station and get the original signal from the carrier wave. The signal is very weak, so the radio amplifies it (makes it louder) before turning it back into sound.

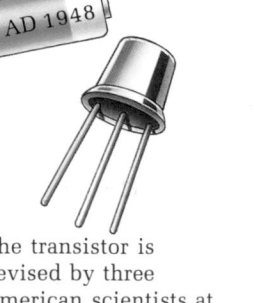

Aerial · Amplifier makes signal much larger · Tuner · Electromagnets make loudspeaker cone vibrate to make sound

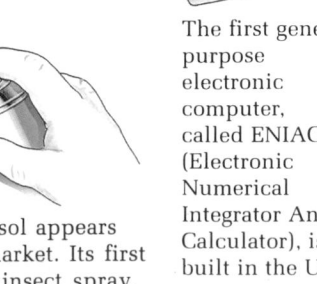

The aerosol appears on the market. Its first use is as insect spray.

The first general-purpose electronic computer, called ENIAC (Electronic Numerical Integrator And Calculator), is built in the USA.

The transistor is devised by three American scientists at the Bell Laboratories in the USA.

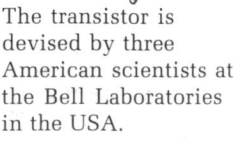

The first experimental colour television broadcasts are made in the USA.

Lenses focus picture on to sensors

Red detector

Green detector

Viewfinder

Mirrors or prisms split colour into red, green and blue parts

Blue detector

Getting the picture

A television shows 25 pictures every second. Each one is slightly different from the one before, which gives the illusion of movement. Each picture is made up of hundreds of closely packed horizontal lines. The television starts at the top of the screen and 'draws' the picture line by line.

Decoding a signal

A television signal tells the television what colours to 'draw', when to go back to start a new line of picture, and when to start a new picture. It also contains the sound to go with the pictures.

Aerial collects television signals

Tuner picks out signals for channel wanted

Electronics decode signal into signals for each electron beam and sound signal.

Electron beams

Screen

Electron guns fire electron beams

Satellite and cable

Satellite television pictures come via satellites in space. You need a special dish-like aerial to collect the signals from the satellite. Many signals are coded so a special decoder is needed. Cable television signals travel along underground cables to your home.

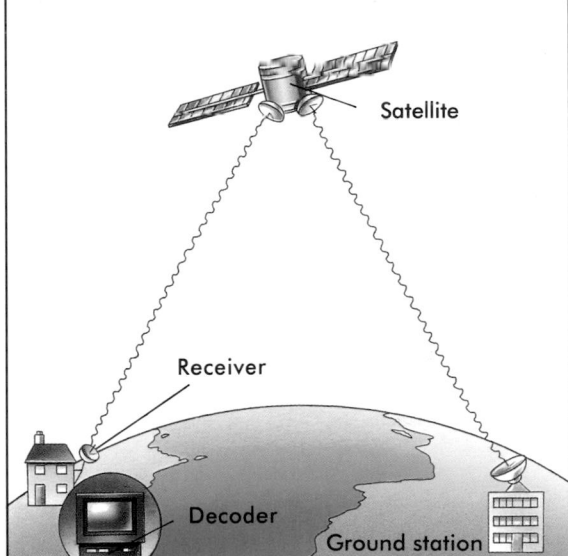

Satellite

Receiver

Decoder

Ground station

Making the picture

A television picture is drawn by a beam of tiny particles called electrons. They hit the back of the screen, making special phosphor dots glow. There are three beams which hit three different colours of dots — red, green and blue. Changing the strength of the beams gives different mixes of red, green and blue to make the colours of the picture.

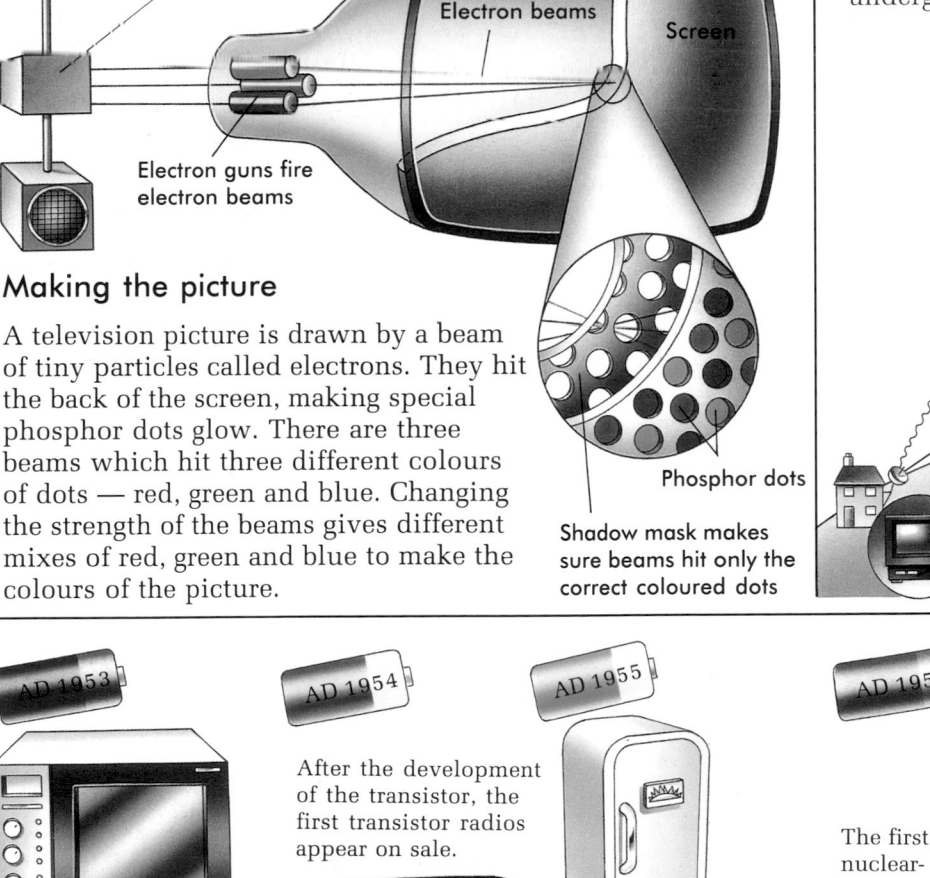

Phosphor dots

Shadow mask makes sure beams hit only the correct coloured dots

AD 1953

The first microwave ovens appear. Domestic microwaves do not appear until the late 1960s.

AD 1954

After the development of the transistor, the first transistor radios appear on sale.

AD 1955

Domestic deep-freeze machines appear in the USA.

AD 1955

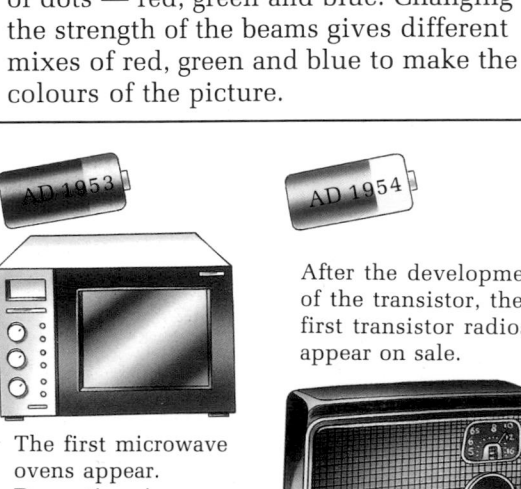

The first nuclear-powered submarine, the *USS Nautilus*, goes into service.

Recording sound and pictures

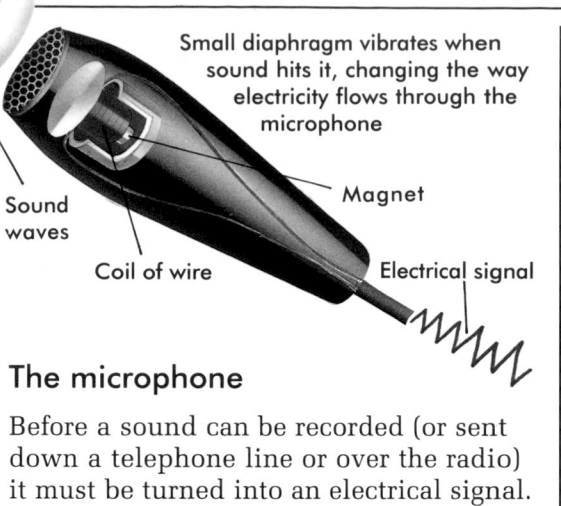

Small diaphragm vibrates when sound hits it, changing the way electricity flows through the microphone

Sound waves

Magnet

Coil of wire

Electrical signal

The microphone

Before a sound can be recorded (or sent down a telephone line or over the radio) it must be turned into an electrical signal. This is the job of a microphone.

Playing back

When recordings are played back, the electrical signals are passed to an amplifier (to make them stronger) and then to loudspeakers. They can be copied to another recording machine or sent to a transmitter to be broadcast.

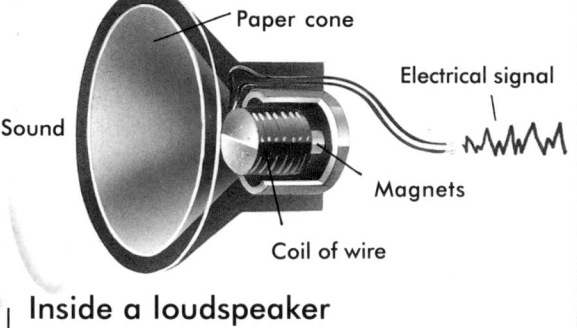

Paper cone

Electrical signal

Sound

Magnets

Coil of wire

Inside a loudspeaker

A loudspeaker does the reverse of a microphone — it turns an electrical signal into sound. The signal goes through a coil of wire which is surrounded by magnets. This makes the coil vibrate in and out, moving a paper cone which makes the sound.

Recordings of pictures and sounds are important for entertainment, for news reporting, and for recording events.

Tape recording

Recording tape is made of flexible plastic with magnetic material in it or coated on one side. An electric current in the recording head makes a magnetic pattern on the tape as it moves past. To play the sound, the tape is moved past a playback head. The magnetic pattern creates an electrical signal in the head, which is used to make sound.

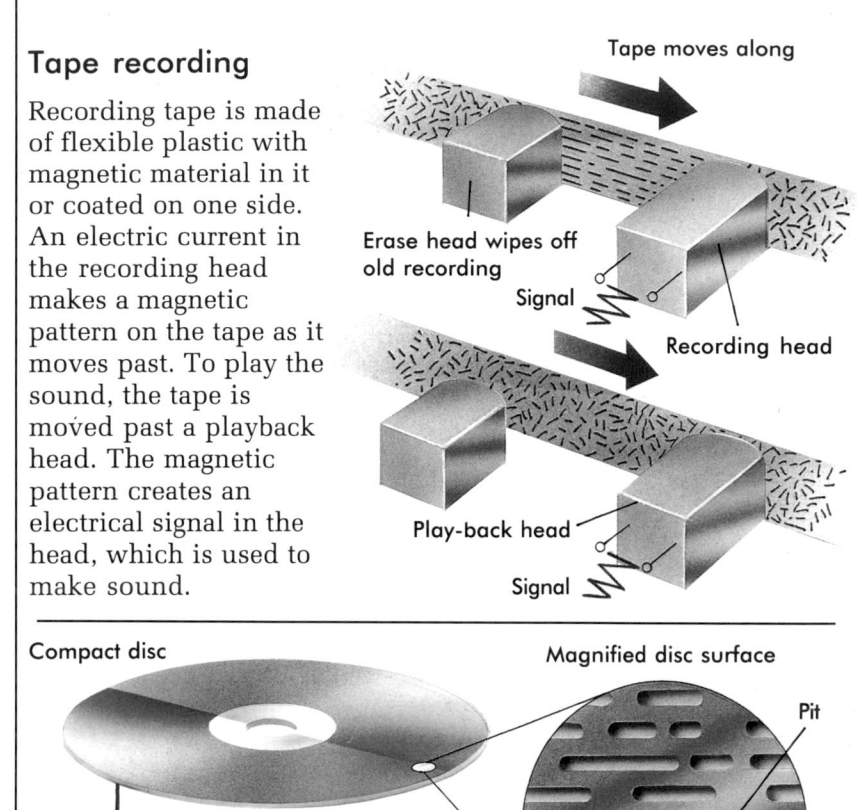

Tape moves along

Erase head wipes off old recording

Signal

Recording head

Play-back head

Signal

Compact disc

Magnified disc surface

Pit

Laser beam moves across disc to follow spiral track

Laser

Flat

Optics detect pits and flats on disc surface

Compact disc

On a compact disc, sound is recorded in digital form. This means that the shape of the signal is recorded as a long list of numbers. To play the sound back, a compact disc player reads the disc and rebuilds the signal. It's a bit like drawing a graph from a list of numbers.

AD 1956 The first video recordings are made. Before this, all television programmes were broadcast live.

c AD 1958 A flexible endoscope using optical fibres is developed.

AD 1958 Stereo records are first sold in Britain and the USA.

AD 1958 Engineers at Texas Instruments in the USA make the first silicon chip.

INTERNET LINK http://www.myweb3000.com
Click on 'Practical Inventions' and try out the puzzles and
other challenging activities.

Taking pictures

Photographic film is coated with special chemicals which change into different chemicals when light hits them. After a film has been exposed to light, it must be developed to make the photograph permanent.

The camera

The job of a camera is to make light fall on a film to record a picture. To do this it must focus the light with a lens, make sure that the right amount of light falls on the film, and keep out unwanted light.

Viewfinder

Flash unit

Film

Lens collects light
and focuses it on to film

Shutter opens to take photograph

Infra-red beam works out distance to object
for automatic focusing

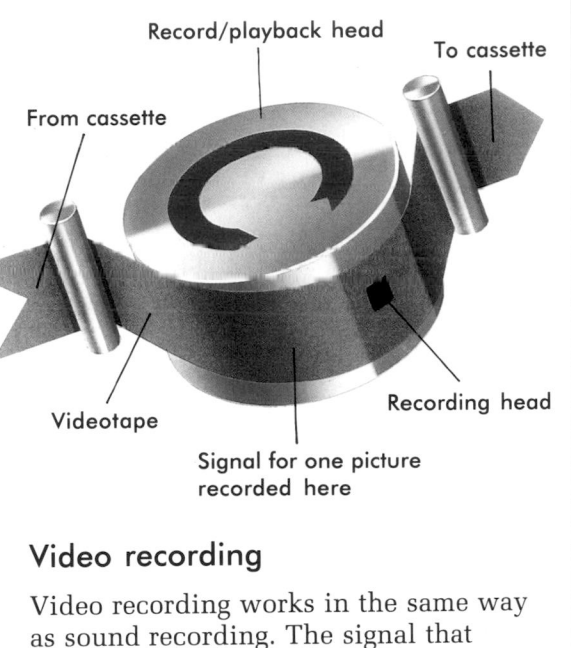

Record/playback head

To cassette

From cassette

Videotape

Recording head

Signal for one picture
recorded here

Video recording

Video recording works in the same way as sound recording. The signal that controls the television is recorded on a magnetic tape. The recording head rotates as the tape goes by, making diagonal tracks across the tape (one for each picture). Moving pictures can also be recorded digitally.

Camcorders

A camcorder is like a camera combined with a video recorder. Instead of film, the camcorder has a special microchip which has thousands of tiny light-sensitive cells on its surface. It divides the picture into thousands of tiny dots of colour and then makes up a video signal which is recorded on the videotape.

Viewfinder has tiny
television set inside

Videocassette

Microphone

Lens

Light-sensitive microchip

Recording head

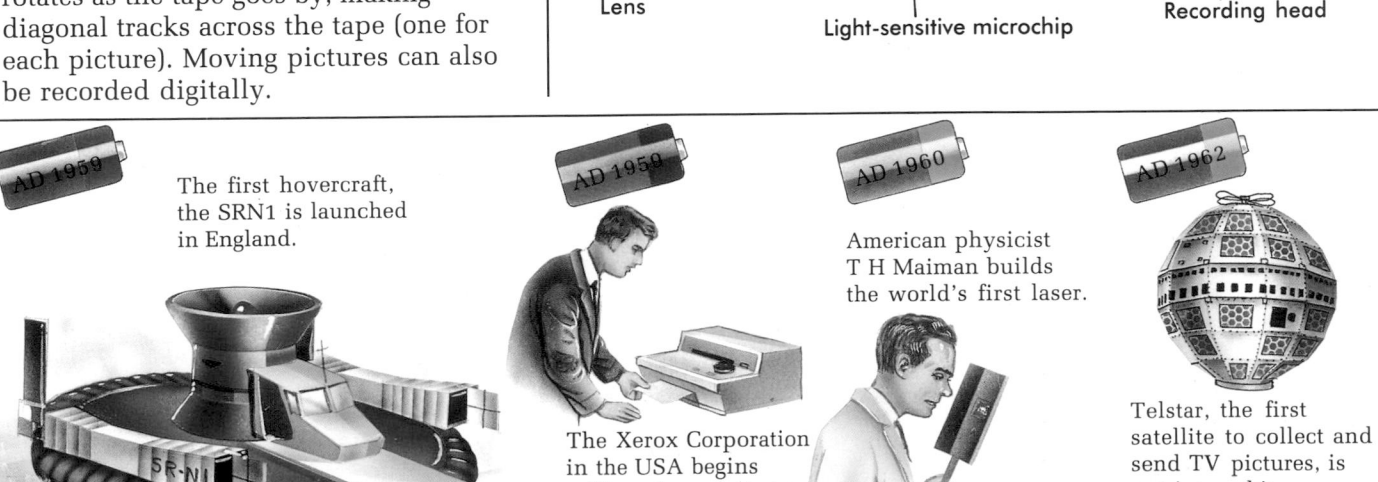

AD 1959

The first hovercraft, the SRN1 is launched in England.

AD 1959

The Xerox Corporation in the USA begins selling photocopiers.

AD 1960

American physicist T H Maiman builds the world's first laser.

AD 1962

Telstar, the first satellite to collect and send TV pictures, is put into orbit.

Science and medicine

Many different machines and instruments are used in the worlds of scientific investigation and medicine. Here you can see how some of them work.

Looking closer

A magnifying glass is the simplest device for investigating things more closely. Its lens works by bending light as it travels to your eye. This makes the object look bigger than it really is.

Rays of light from object

Image — this is where the object appears to be

Object

Listen carefully

Your doctor listens to your heartbeat and breathing with a stethoscope. It picks up vibrations from your body and turns them into sound. The sound travels along tubes to the doctor's ears.

Thin diaphragm picks up vibrations inside body

Sound travels along tubes

Spectacles

Spectacles correct defects in people's eyes. They contain lenses which bend the light going into an eye so that it focuses properly on the retina. Contact lenses do the same job.

Short sightedness

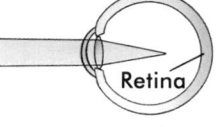

Retina

Image formed in front of retina

Spectacle lens (concave)

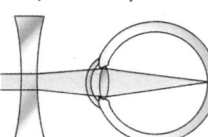

Long sightedness

Image formed behind retina

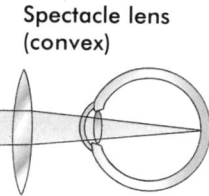

Spectacle lens (convex)

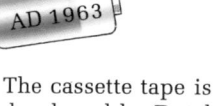

And closer still

A microscope uses two or more lenses. The image made by the first lens (called the objective lens) is magnified again by another lens (called the eye piece). Microscopes can magnify things up to about two thousand times.

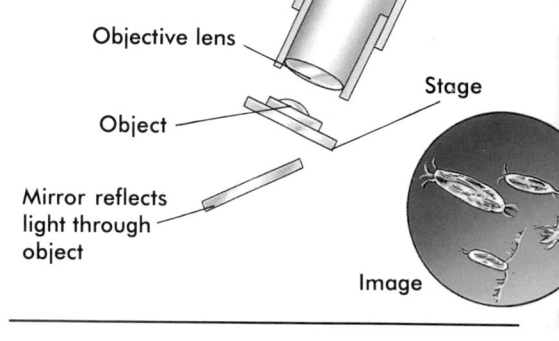

Eye piece

Objective lens

Object

Stage

Mirror reflects light through object

Image

Million magnifiers

Easily the most powerful magnifying machines are electron microscopes. A transmission electron microscope fires a beam of tiny particles called electrons through a thin slice of an object. Magnets focus the beam on to a screen (like a television) to make an image. Some electron microscopes can magnify things many million times.

Gun fires electron beam

Object goes here

Magnets focus beam

Image made here

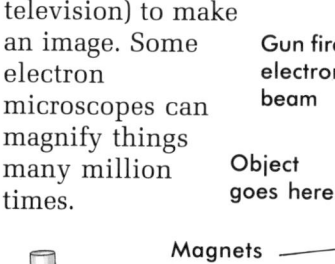

AD 1960s

The RCA company in the USA invents the musical synthesiser, which makes sounds artificially.

AD 1962

American company Unimation markets the first simple industrial robot.

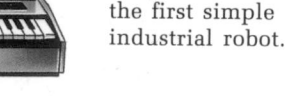

AD 1963

The cassette tape is developed by Dutch company Philips.

AD 1966

Scientists realise that telephone calls could be sent along optical fibres as pulses of light.

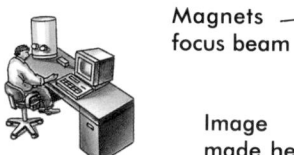

INTERNET LINK http://www.inventorsmuseum.com
Check out past inventions as well as the latest creations, then take the Inventor's IQ text.

Tube viewer

An endoscope is a thin flexible tube that surgeons use to see inside a patient's body. The picture travels along a bundle of optical fibres with a lens at each end. Light is sent down another optical fibre to help the surgeon see. An endoscope tube sometimes contains wires to operate tiny surgical instruments at its end.

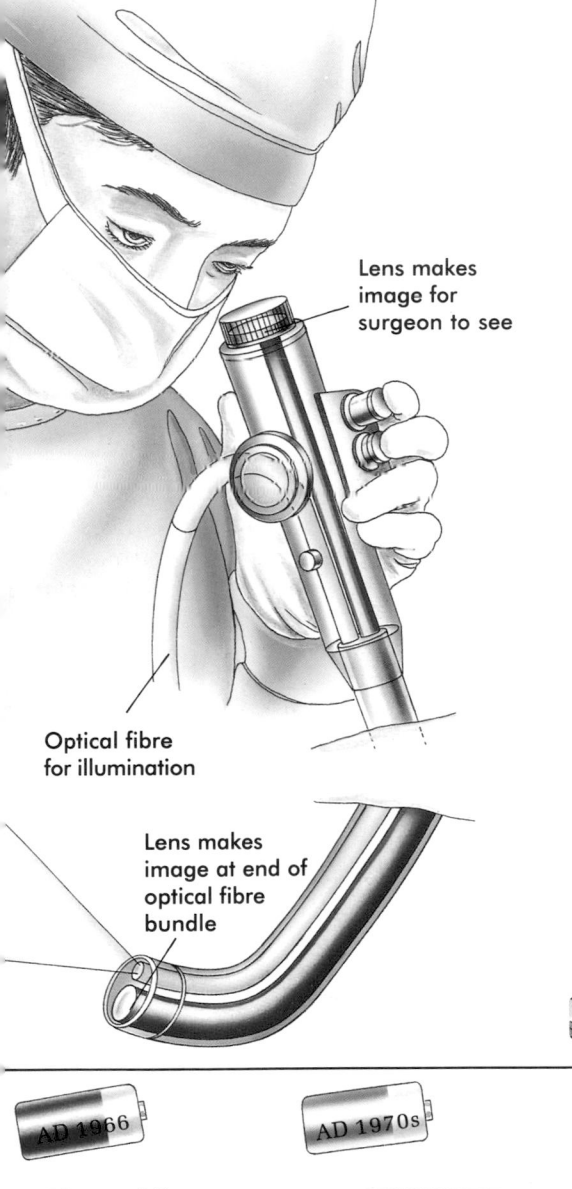

Lens makes image for surgeon to see

Optical fibre for illumination

Lens makes image at end of optical fibre bundle

X-ray pictures

An X-ray machine takes a photograph of the inside of your body. The machine fires a beam of X-rays at a piece of photographic film. The part of the patient's body to be looked at is put in front of the film. Dense parts of the body, such as bones, absorb the X-rays more than less dense parts. This makes a sort of shadow picture on the film.

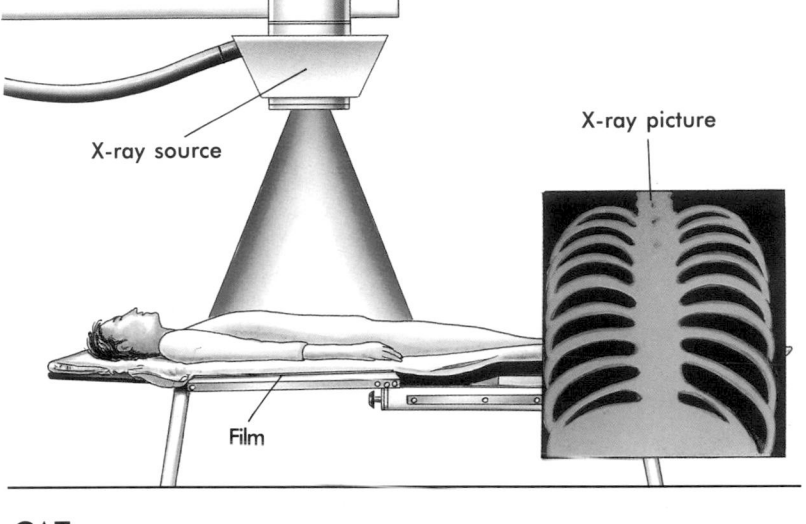

X-ray source

X-ray picture

Film

CAT scans

CAT stands for computerised axial tomography. A CAT scanner is a special type of X-ray machine. It scans a slice of a patient's body with X-rays. A computer builds up a 3-D picture of the inside of the patient's body slice by slice.

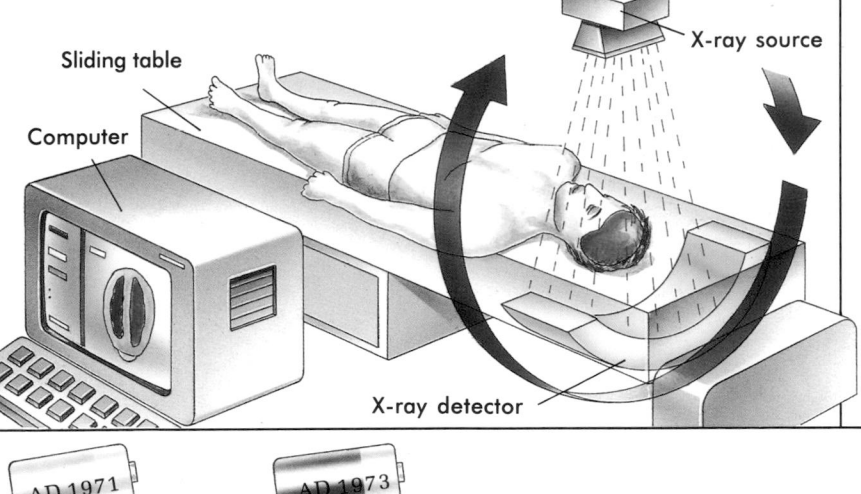

Sliding table

Computer

X-ray source

X-ray detector

AD 1966

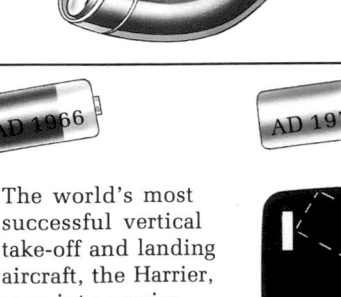

The world's most successful vertical take-off and landing aircraft, the Harrier, goes into service.

AD 1970s

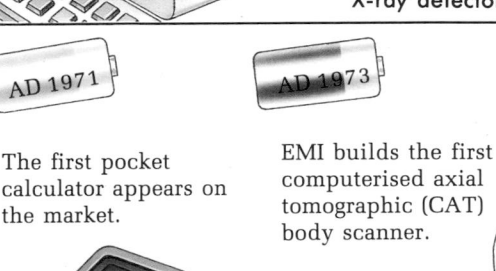

Simple ping-pong style computer games appear.

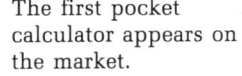AD 1971

The first pocket calculator appears on the market.

AD 1973

EMI builds the first computerised axial tomographic (CAT) body scanner.

Into space

There are thousands of man-made things in space. Most of them are in orbit around the Earth. They are put there by rocket-powered launch vehicles.

Engines for space

Spacecraft use rocket engines. All engines that burn fuel need a supply of oxygen. Most engines get their oxygen from the Earth's atmosphere. But there is no atmosphere in space, so rocket engines have to carry their own supply of oxygen. The fuel and oxygen supply are mixed together and burnt. This sends a stream of hot gases rushing out of the engine, pushing the engine forwards.

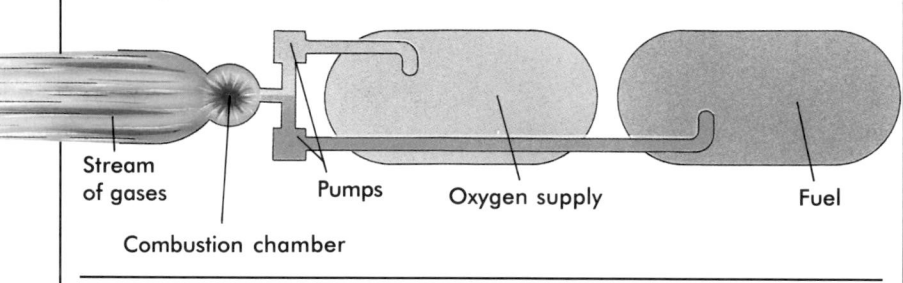

Stream of gases

Combustion chamber

Pumps

Oxygen supply

Fuel

Staying in space

Satellites stay in space above the Earth because they are in orbit. They move along a very long path around the Earth. The Earth's gravity stops a satellite disappearing into space and the satellite's speed stops it falling back to Earth. Once the satellite is moving it keeps moving because there is no air trying to slow it down.

Putting a satellite into orbit is like throwing it from an extremely tall tower. Throw the satellite lightly and it falls to the ground. But throw it fast enough and it never reaches the ground.

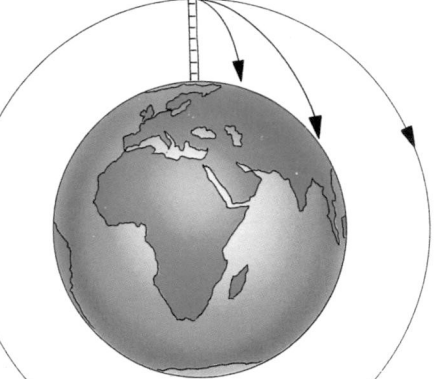

Path of orbit

Getting into orbit

Satellites are put into orbit by launch vehicles. A launch vehicle lifts the satellite out of the Earth's atmosphere and sends it along the path of its orbit. A launch vehicle normally has three stages. As each stage runs out of fuel it is jettisoned and the next stage takes over.

Satellite in protective cover

Third stage engine

Second stage engine

Fuel and oxygen tanks

First stage engine

Third stage takes satellite into orbit

Second stage takes over

First stage burns

Satellites

Communication satellites must stay in orbit, aim their antennae at Earth, and keep working for years on end. They have thrusters (like tiny rocket engines) to make small changes in position.
Electric power comes from solar panels, which turn sunlight into electricity.

Antennae

Solar panels

AD 1977

A cellular telephone is demonstrated for the first time.

AD 1979

In Japan, a maglev (magnetic levitation) train carries passengers for the first time.

AD 1981

The first US Space Shuttle, *Columbia*, lifts off for its maiden flight.

AD 1981

IBM introduces the first personal business computer.

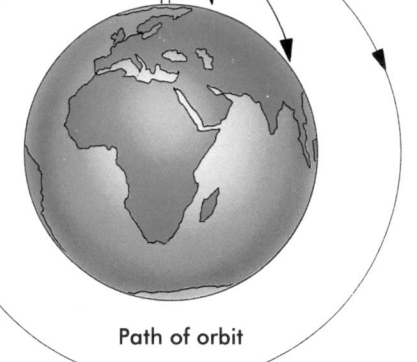

INTERNET LINK http://express.howstuffworks.com
This site is constantly updated to include a variety of topical articles, plus exciting theories on inventions of the future.

Up and back

The Space Shuttle is a partly reusable launch vehicle. The Shuttle uses booster rockets during the first part of its flight into space. After its mission, the orbiter glides back to Earth like an aircraft.

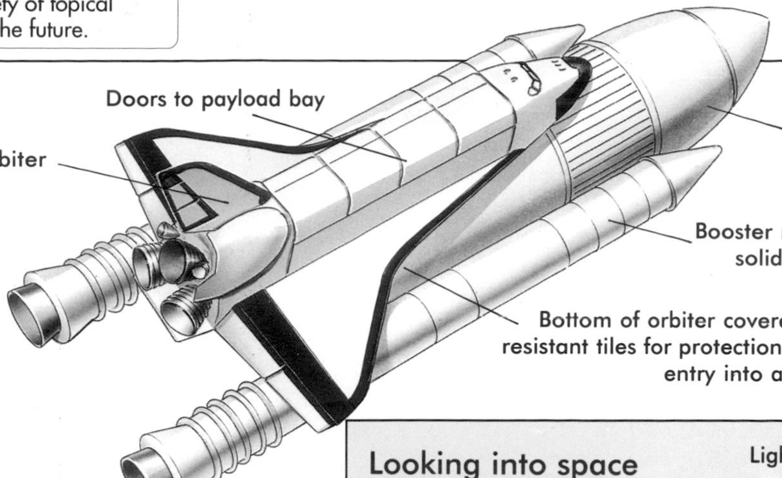

Doors to payload bay
Orbiter
Fuel tank for orbiter engines
Booster rockets use solid rocket fuel
Bottom of orbiter covered in heat-resistant tiles for protection during re-entry into atmosphere

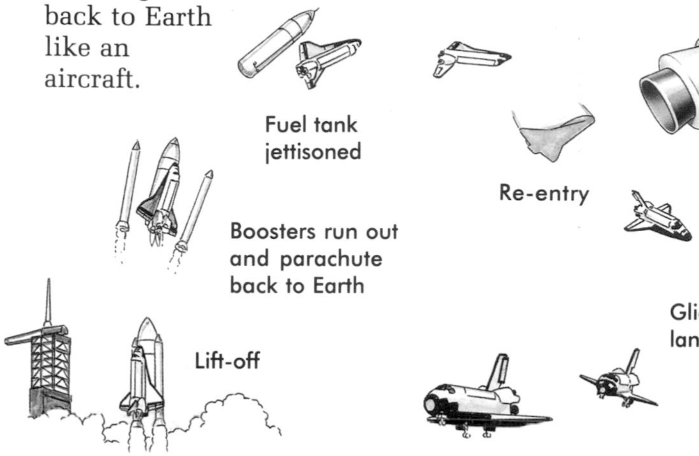

Fuel tank jettisoned
Re-entry
Boosters run out and parachute back to Earth
Glide to landing
Lift-off

Suits for space

Astronauts wear spacesuits when they leave their spacecraft. The suit has two parts. The inner part is a thin rubber bladder. It contains air for the astronaut to breathe and stops the astronaut's blood boiling (which would happen because there is no air pressure in space). The outer part protects against radiation from the Sun and tiny meteorites. The backpack contains oxygen for breathing and water for cooling.

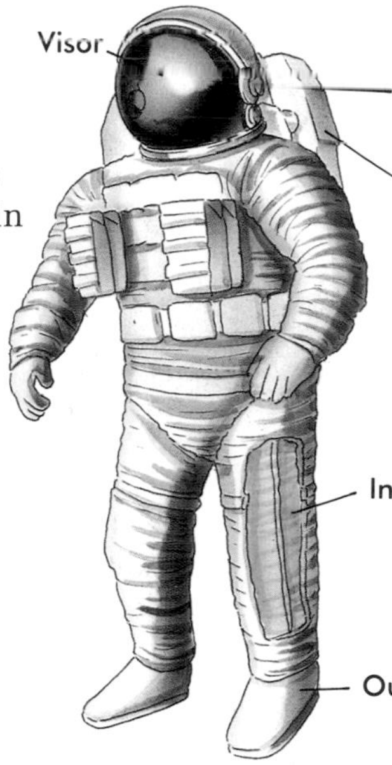

Visor
Helmet
Backpack
Inner layer
Outer layer

Looking into space

Telescopes are used to make distant objects look much bigger. Most astronomical telescopes are called reflecting telescopes because they use a large mirror to make an image. The image can be seen through an eye piece, recorded with a camera, or measured with electronic equipment.

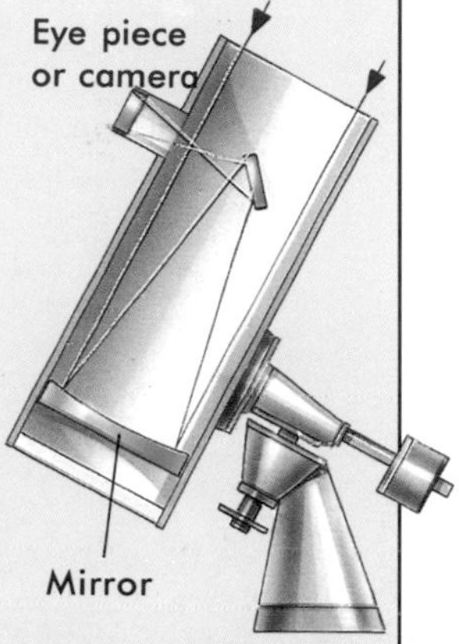

Light from star
Eye piece or camera
Mirror
Pivots move telescope to aim at any part of sky

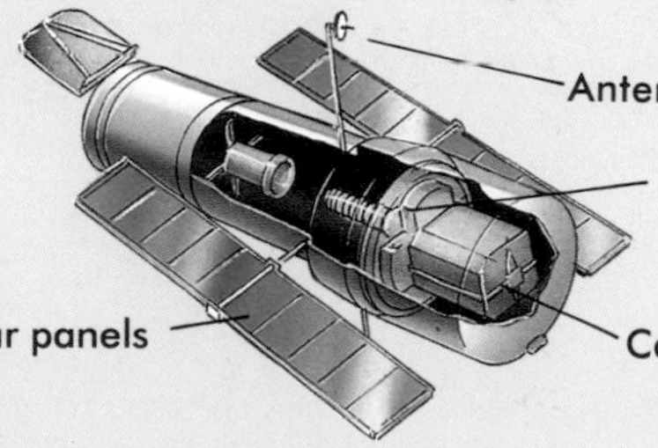

Antenna
Mirror
Solar panels
Camera

The Earth's atmosphere makes pictures seen by telescopes on Earth look slightly blurred. The Hubble Space Telescope is a reflecting telescope in space. It can see stars much more clearly than telescopes on Earth. The pictures are seen by an electronic detector and sent down to Earth by radio.

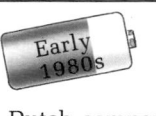

Early 1980s

Dutch company Philips introduces the compact disc, which begins to replace records and cassettes.

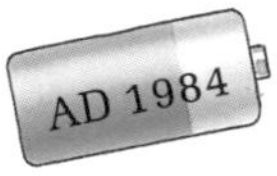

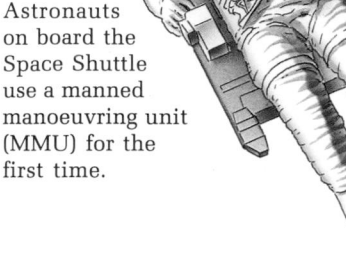

AD 1984

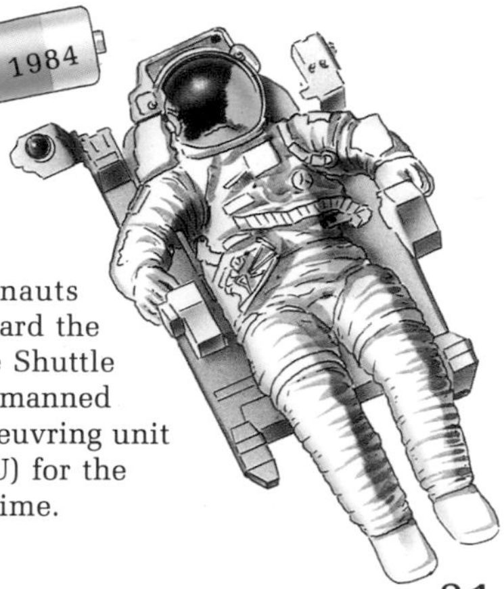

Astronauts on board the Space Shuttle use a manned manoeuvring unit (MMU) for the first time.

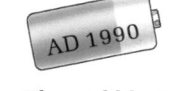

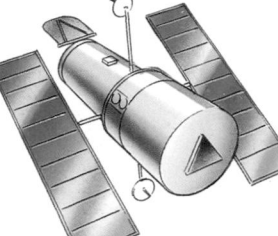

AD 1990

The Hubble Space Telescope is put into orbit by the Space Shuttle.

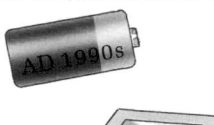

AD 1990s

The global positioning system of navigation satellites is completed.

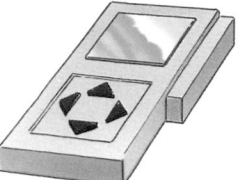

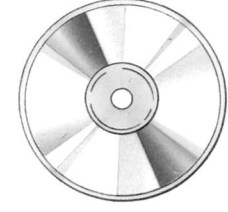

Index

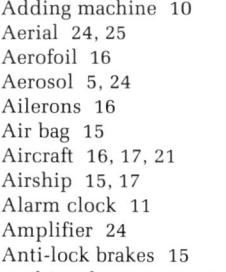